A Midsummer Night's Dream

....

William Shakespeare

PRENTICE HALL
Upper Saddle River, New Jersey
Needham, Massachusetts

Publishing History

A Midsummer Night's Dream was first published in 1600.

ISBN   0-13-435469-9

2 3 4 5 6 7 8 9 10   02 01 00 99

PRENTICE HALL
Simon & Schuster Education Group

CHARACTERS

Hermia
Lysander } *four lovers*
Helena
Demetrius

Theseus, duke of Athens

Hippolyta, queen of the Amazons

Egeus, father to Hermia

Philostrate, master of the revels to Theseus

Nick Bottom, weaver

Peter Quince, carpenter

Francis Flute, bellows-mender

Tom Snout, tinker

Snug, joiner

Robin Starveling, tailor

Oberon, king of the Fairies

Titania, queen of the Fairies

Robin Goodfellow, a "puck," or hobgoblin, in
Oberon's service

A Fairy, in the service of Titania

Peaseblossom
Cobweb } *fairies attending upon Titania*
Mote
Mustardseed

Lords and Attendants on Theseus and Hippolyta

Other Fairies in the trains of Titania and Oberon

1

Act I

Scene i. *Enter Theseus, Hippolyta, and Philostrate,*
with others.

THESEUS.
    Now, fair Hippolyta, our nuptial hour
    Draws on apace. Four happy days bring in
    Another moon. But, O, methinks how slow
    This old moon wanes! She lingers[1] my desires
5   Like to a stepdame or a dowager
    Long withering out a young man's revenue.[2]

HIPPOLYTA.
    Four days will quickly steep themselves in night;
    Four nights will quickly dream away the time;
    And then the moon, like to a silver bow
10   New-bent in heaven, shall behold the night
    Of our solemnities.

THESEUS.   Go, Philostrate,
    Stir up the Athenian youth to merriments.
    Awake the pert and nimble spirit of mirth.
15   Turn melancholy forth to funerals;
    The pale companion[3] is not for our pomp.

                    Philostrate exits.

    Hippolyta, I wooed thee with my sword[4]
    And won thy love doing thee injuries,
    But I will wed thee in another key,
20   With pomp, with triumph, and with reveling.

    Enter Egeus and his daughter Hermia, and
        Lysander and Demetrius.

---

1. lingers: Is slow to leave; delays.
2. Like . . . revenue: This describes an older woman—stepmother or widow—
who controls and perhaps uses up a young man's money.
3. companion: *Companion* literally means "fellow" and is used here to indicate
contempt.
4. I . . . sword: Hippolyta was courted by the soldier Theseus during his battles
with her people, the Amazons.

EGEUS.
Happy be Theseus, our renownèd duke!

THESEUS.
Thanks, good Egeus. What's the news with thee?

EGEUS.
Full of vexation come I, with complaint
Against my child, my daughter Hermia.—
25 Stand forth, Demetrius.—My noble lord,
This man hath my consent to marry her.—
Stand forth, Lysander.—And, my gracious duke,
This man hath bewitched the bosom of my child.—
Thou, thou, Lysander, thou hast given her rhymes
30 And interchanged love tokens with my child.
Thou hast by moonlight at her window sung
With feigning voice verses of feigning love[5]
And stol'n the impression of her fantasy[6]
With bracelets of thy hair, rings, gauds, conceits,
35 Knacks,[7] trifles, nosegays, sweetmeats—messen-
gers
Of strong prevailment[8] in unhardened youth.
With cunning hast thou filched my daughter's
heart,
40 Turned her obedience which is due to me
To stubborn harshness.—And, my gracious duke,
Be it so[9] she will not here before your Grace
Consent to marry with Demetrius,
I beg the ancient privilege of Athens:
45 As she is mine, I may dispose of her,
Which shall be either to this gentleman
Or to her death, according to our law
Immediately[10] provided in that case.

---

5. With . . . feigning love: A quiet voice singing of false or pretended love.
6. And . . . her fantasy: Used trickery and dishonesty to leave your mark upon her imagination.
7. gauds, conceits,/Knacks: Fancy toys or playthings; trinkets or baubles; knickknacks.
8. prevailment: Impact; effect.
9. Be it so: If.
10. Immediately: Particularly; especially.

THESEUS.
What say you, Hermia? Be advised, fair maid.
50   To you, your father should be as a god,
One that composed your beauties, yea, and one
To whom you are but as a form in wax
By him imprinted, and within his power
To leave[11] the figure or disfigure it.
55   Demetrius is a worthy gentleman.

HERMIA.
So is Lysander.

THESEUS.   In himself he is,
But in this kind, wanting your father's voice,[12]
The other must be held the worthier.

HERMIA.
60   I would my father looked but with my eyes.

THESEUS.
Rather your eyes must with his judgment look.

HERMIA.
I do entreat your Grace to pardon me.
I know not by what power I am made bold,
Nor how it may concern my modesty[13]
65   In such a presence here to plead my thoughts;
But I beseech your Grace that I may know
The worst that may befall me in this case
If I refuse to wed Demetrius.

THESEUS.
Either to die the death, or to abjure
70   Forever the society of men.
Therefore, fair Hermia, question your desires,
Know of your youth, examine well your blood,[14]
Whether if you yield not to your father's choice
You can endure the livery of a nun,
75   For aye to be in shady cloister mewed,

11. **leave:** Leave unchanged.
12. **But in . . . father's voice:** In this situation, lacking your father's consent.
13. **concern my modesty:** Suit my reputation for modest, proper behavior.
14. **blood:** Passionate feelings.

4

To live a barren sister all your life,[15]
Chanting faint hymns to the cold fruitless moon.[16]
Thrice-blessèd they that master so their blood
To undergo such maiden pilgrimage,
80   But earthlier happy is the rose distilled[17]
Than that which, withering on the virgin thorn,
Grows, lives, and dies in single blessedness.

HERMIA.
So will I grow, so live, so die, my lord,
Ere I will yield my virgin patent[18] up
85   Unto his lordship whose unwished yoke
My soul consents not to give sovereignty.

THESEUS.
Take time to pause, and by the next new moon
The sealing day betwixt my love and me
For everlasting bond of fellowship,
90   Upon that day either prepare to die
For disobedience to your father's will,
Or else to wed Demetrius, as he would,
Or on Diana's altar to protest[19]
For aye austerity and single life.

DEMETRIUS.
95   Relent, sweet Hermia, and, Lysander, yield
Thy crazèd title[20] to my certain right.

LYSANDER.
You have her father's love, Demetrius.
Let me have Hermia's. Do you marry him.

EGEUS.
Scornful Lysander, true, he hath my love;
100   And what is mine my love shall render him.

15. You can . . . your life: Live as a chaste nun, in special clothing, separated for always from the world.
16. moon: Reference to Diana, the goddess of the moon and of chastity.
17. But earthlier . . . distilled: The married woman, whose beauty has been plucked from its natural state and distilled into perfume, will be happier on Earth than those who live their lives in chastity, or single blessedness.
18. patent: Right or privilege.
19. protest: Commit to; promise.
20. crazèd title: Unsound claim or title.

And she is mine, and all my right of her
I do estate unto[21] Demetrius.

LYSANDER. *(to Theseus)*
    I am, my lord, as well derived[22] as he,
    As well possessed.[23] My love is more than his;
105   My fortunes every way as fairly ranked
    If not with vantage[24] as Demetrius';
    And which is more than all these boasts can be
    I am beloved of beauteous Hermia.
    Why should not I then prosecute my right?
110   Demetrius, I'll avouch it to his head,[25]
    Made love to Nedar's daughter, Helena,
    And won her soul; and she, sweet lady, dotes,
    Devoutly dotes, dotes in idolatry,
    Upon this spotted[26] and inconstant man.

THESEUS.
115   I must confess that I have heard so much,
    And with Demetrius thought to have spoke thereof;
    But, being overfull of self-affairs,[27]
    My mind did lose it.—But, Demetrius, come,
    And come, Egeus; you shall go with me.
120   I have some private schooling[28] for you both.—
    For you, fair Hermia, look you arm[29] yourself
    To fit your fancies to your father's will,
    Or else the law of Athens yields you up
    Which by no means we may extenuate[30]
125   To death or to a vow of single life.—
    Come, my Hippolyta. What cheer, my love?—
    Demetrius and Egeus, go along.
    I must employ you in some business

---

21. estate unto: Give to.
22. well derived: Highly born.
23. well possessed: Rich; wealthy.
24. fairly . . . vantage: As good or better than.
25. to his head: To his face.
26. spotted: Corrupt; morally flawed.
27. self-affairs: My own business.
28. schooling: Advice; warning; reproof.
29. arm: Prepare.
30. extenuate: Modify.

Against[31] our nuptial, and confer with you
130 Of something nearly that[32] concerns yourselves.

EGEUS.
With duty and desire we follow you.

All but Hermia and Lysander exit.

LYSANDER.
How now, my love? Why is your cheek so pale?
How chance the roses there do fade so fast?

HERMIA.
Belike[33] for want of rain, which I could well
135 Beteem[34] them from the tempest of my eyes.

LYSANDER.
Ay me! For aught that I could ever read,
Could ever hear by tale or history,
The course of true love never did run smooth.
But either it was different in blood—[35]

HERMIA.
140 O cross![36] Too high to be enthralled to low.

LYSANDER.
Or else misgraffèd in respect of years—[37]

HERMIA.
O spite! Too old to be engaged to young.

LYSANDER.
Or else it stood upon the choice of friends—[38]

HERMIA.
O hell, to choose love by another's eyes!

LYSANDER.
145 Or, if there were a sympathy in choice,

31. Against: Concerning; in preparation for.
32. nearly that: That closely.
33. Belike: Probably.
34. Beteem: Give; produce for.
35. different in blood: Of unequal hereditary status.
36. cross: Obstacle; problem.
37. misgraffèd . . . years: Of different ages.
38. stood . . . friends: Was chosen by relatives.

War, death, or sickness did lay siege to it,
Making it momentany[39] as a sound,
Swift as a shadow, short as any dream,
Brief as the lightning in the collied[40] night,
150   That, in a spleen, unfolds[41] both heaven and earth,
And, ere a man hath power to say "Behold!"
The jaws of darkness do devour it up.
So quick bright things come to confusion.[42]

HERMIA.
If then true lovers have been ever crossed,[43]
155   It stands as an edict in destiny.
Then let us teach our trial patience[44]
Because it is a customary cross,
As due to love as thoughts and dreams and sighs,
Wishes and tears, poor fancy's[45] followers.

LYSANDER.
160   A good persuasion.[46] Therefore, hear me, Hermia:
I have a widow aunt, a dowager
Of great revenue, and she hath no child.
From Athens is her house remote seven leagues,
And she respects me as her only son.
165   There, gentle Hermia, may I marry thee;
And to that place the sharp Athenian law
Cannot pursue us. If thou lovest me, then
Steal forth thy father's house tomorrow night,
And in the wood a league without the town
170   Where I did meet thee once with Helena
To do observance to a morn of May,[47]
There will I stay for thee.

HERMIA.   My good Lysander,
I swear to thee by Cupid's strongest bow,

39. momentany: Lasting only for a moment.
40. collied: Black like coal.
41. That, in . . . unfolds: The lightning suddenly and unexpectedly reveals.
42. quick . . . confusion: Living and beautiful things quickly meet ruin and disaster.
43. ever crossed: Always facing problems.
44. teach . . . patience: Practice until we learn to be patient.
45. fancy's: Love's.
46. persuasion: Approach; philosophy.
47. To do . . . of May: To celebrate spring, as with May Day.

175 By his best arrow with the golden head,[48]
By the simplicity[49] of Venus' doves,[50]
By that which knitteth souls and prospers loves,
And by that fire which burned the Carthage queen
When the false Trojan under sail was seen,[51]
180 By all the vows that ever men have broke
In number more than ever women spoke,
In that same place thou hast appointed me,
Tomorrow truly will I meet with thee.

LYSANDER.
Keep promise, love. Look, here comes Helena.

Enter Helena.

HERMIA.
185 Godspeed, fair Helena. Whither away?

HELENA.
Call you me "fair"? That "fair" again unsay.
Demetrius loves your fair.[52] O happy fair!
Your eyes are lodestars[53] and your tongue's sweet
air[54]
190 More tunable[55] than lark to shepherd's ear
When wheat is green, when hawthorn buds appear.
Sickness is catching. O, were favor[56] so!
Yours would I catch, fair Hermia, ere I go.
My ear should catch your voice, my eye your eye;
195 My tongue should catch your tongue's sweet
melody.
Were the world mine, Demetrius being bated,

48. best arrow ... golden head: Cupid's best—golden-tipped—arrow caused love, while those with leaden tips caused dislike.
49. simplicity: Purity; innocence.
50. Venus' doves: Those who drew the love goddess's chariot.
51. And by ... was seen: Dido, the Carthage queen, burned herself on a pyre in despair when the false Trojan, Aeneas, deserted her.
52. fair: Beauty.
53. lodestars: Guiding stars.
54. air: Music.
55. tunable: Pleasant sounding.
56. favor: Appearance, especially beauty.

The rest I'd give to be to you translated.[57]
O, teach me how you look and with what art
200   You sway the motion of Demetrius' heart!

HERMIA.

I frown upon him, yet he loves me still.

HELENA.

O, that your frowns would teach my smiles such
skill!

HERMIA.

I give him curses, yet he gives me love.

HELENA.

205   O, that my prayers could such affection move!

HERMIA.

The more I hate, the more he follows me.

HELENA.

The more I love, the more he hateth me.

HERMIA.

His folly, Helena, is no fault of mine.

HELENA.

None but your beauty. Would that fault were mine!

HERMIA.

210   Take comfort: he no more shall see my face.
Lysander and myself will fly this place.
Before the time I did Lysander see
Seemed Athens as a paradise to me.
O, then, what graces in my love do dwell
215   That he hath turned a heaven unto a hell!

LYSANDER.

Helen, to you our minds we will unfold.
Tomorrow night when Phoebe[58] doth behold
Her silver visage in the wat'ry glass,[59]
Decking with liquid pearl the bladed grass

---

57. **Demetrius . . . translated:** Except for Demetrius, I'd give anything to be
transformed into you.
58. **Phoebe:** Diana, goddess of the moon.
59. **glass:** Mirror; here created by a body of water.

220   A time that lovers' flights doth still[60] conceal,
    Through Athens' gates have we devised to steal.

HERMIA.
    And in the wood where often you and I
    Upon faint[61] primrose beds were wont to lie,
    Emptying our bosoms of their counsel sweet,
225   There my Lysander and myself shall meet,
    And thence from Athens turn away our eyes
    To seek new friends and stranger companies.[62]
    Farewell, sweet playfellow. Pray thou for us,
    And good luck grant thee thy Demetrius.—
230   Keep word, Lysander. We must starve our sight
    From lovers' food till morrow deep midnight.

LYSANDER.
    I will, my Hermia.   *(Hermia exits.)*
             Helena, adieu.
    As you on him, Demetrius dote on you!

                      Lysander exits.

HELENA.
235   How happy some o'er other some can be![63]
    Through Athens I am thought as fair as she.
    But what of that? Demetrius thinks not so.
    He will not know what all but he do know.
    And, as he errs, doting on Hermia's eyes,
240   So I, admiring of his qualities.
    Things base and vile, holding no quantity,[64]
    Love can transpose to form and dignity.
    Love looks not with the eyes but with the mind;
    And therefore is winged Cupid painted blind.
245   Nor hath Love's mind of any judgment taste.[65]
    Wings, and no eyes, figure[66] unheedy haste.
    And therefore is Love said to be a child

60. still: Always.
61. faint: Pallid.
62. stranger companies: Strangers as companions.
63. some o'er . . . be: Some more than others.
64. holding no quantity: Not in proportion, thus unattractive.
65. Nor . . . judgment taste: Love, which arises from feelings, is without judgment.
66. figure: Symbolize.

Because in choice he is so oft beguiled.
As waggish boys in game themselves forswear,[67]
250 So the boy Love is perjured everywhere.
For, ere Demetrius looked on Hermia's eyne,[68]
He hailed down oaths that he was only mine;
And when this hail some heat from Hermia felt,
So he dissolved, and show'rs of oaths did melt.
255 I will go tell him of fair Hermia's flight.
Then to the wood will he tomorrow night
Pursue her. And, for this intelligence[69]
If I have thanks, it is a dear expense.[70]
But herein mean I to enrich my pain,
260 To have his sight thither and back again.

She exits.

Scene ii. *Enter Quince the carpenter, and Snug the joiner, and Bottom the weaver, and Flute the bellows-mender, and Snout the tinker, and Starveling the tailor.*

QUINCE. Is all our company here?

BOTTOM. You were best to call them generally,[1] man by man, according to the scrip.[2]

QUINCE. Here is the scroll of every man's name which is
5 thought fit, through all Athens, to play in our interlude[3] before the Duke and the Duchess on his wedding day at night.

BOTTOM. First, good Peter Quince, say what the play treats on, then read the names of the actors, and
10 so grow to a point.[4]

---

67. **waggish . . . forswear:** As playful boys pretend or swear falsely during sports or pranks.
68. **eyne:** Eyes.
69. **intelligence:** Information; news.
70. **a dear expense:** An effort worth making; a costly effort.
1. **generally:** Bottom actually means "individually."
2. **scrip:** Bottom actually means "script."
3. **interlude:** A dramatic entertainment.
4. **grow to a point:** Reach a conclusion.

QUINCE. Marry,[5] our play is "The most lamentable comedy and most cruel death of Pyramus and Thisbe."[6]

BOTTOM. A very good piece of work, I assure you, and a merry. Now, good Peter Quince, call forth your actors by the scroll. Masters, spread yourselves.

15

QUINCE. Answer as I call you. Nick Bottom, the weaver.

BOTTOM. Ready. Name what part I am for, and proceed.

QUINCE. You, Nick Bottom, are set down for Pyramus.

BOTTOM. What is Pyramus—a lover or a tyrant?

20 **QUINCE.** A lover that kills himself most gallant for love.

BOTTOM. That will ask some tears in the true performing of it. If I do it, let the audience look to their eyes. I will move storms; I will condole[7] in some measure. To the rest.—Yet my chief humor[8] is for a
25 tyrant. I could play Ercles[9] rarely, or a part to tear a cat in,[10] to make all split:

> The raging rocks
> And shivering shocks
> Shall break the locks
30 > Of prison gates.
> And Phibbus' car[11]
> Shall shine from far
> And make and mar
> The foolish Fates.

35 This was lofty. Now name the rest of the players. This is Ercles' vein, a tyrant's vein. A lover is more condoling.

QUINCE. Francis Flute, the bellows-mender.

---

5. Marry: Derived from the mild oath "By the Virgin Mary."
6. Pyramus and Thisbe: A classical tale, similar to that of Romeo and Juliet.
7. condole: Mourn, perhaps in the part of the grieving lover.
8. humor: Temperament; inclination.
9. Ercles: Hercules, a character known for ranting.
10. to tear a cat in: Rant and rave.
11. Phibbus' car: The chariot of Phoebus Apollo, the sun god.

FLUTE. Here, Peter Quince.

40   **QUINCE.** Flute, you must take Thisbe on you.

FLUTE. What is Thisbe—a wand'ring knight?

QUINCE. It is the lady that Pyramus must love.

FLUTE. Nay, faith, let not me play a woman. I have a beard coming.

45   **QUINCE.** That's all one.[12] You shall play it in a mask, and you may speak as small[13] as you will.

BOTTOM. An[14] I may hide my face, let me play Thisbe too. I'll speak in a monstrous little voice: "Thisne, Thisne!"—"Ah Pyramus, my lover dear! Thy Thisbe
50   dear and lady dear!"

QUINCE. No, no, you must play Pyramus—and, Flute, you Thisbe.

BOTTOM. Well, proceed.

QUINCE. Robin Starveling, the tailor.

55   **STARVELING.** Here, Peter Quince.

QUINCE. Robin Starveling, you must play Thisbe's mother.—Tom Snout, the tinker.

SNOUT. Here, Peter Quince.

QUINCE. You, Pyramus' father.—Myself, Thisbe's father.
60   —Snug the joiner, you the lion's part.—And I hope here is a play fitted.

SNUG. Have you the lion's part written? Pray you, if it be, give it me, for I am slow of study.

QUINCE. You may do it extempore, for it is nothing but
65   roaring.

BOTTOM. Let me play the lion too. I will roar that I will

---

12. **That's all one:** That doesn't matter.
13. **small:** Softly and in the higher pitch of a woman's voice.
14. **An:** If.

do any man's heart good to hear me. I will roar that I will make the Duke say "Let him roar again. Let him roar again!"

70   **QUINCE.** An you should do it too terribly, you would fright the Duchess and the ladies that they would shriek, and that were enough to hang us all.

ALL. That would hang us, every mother's son.

BOTTOM. I grant you, friends, if you should fright the
75   ladies out of their wits, they would have no more discretion but to hang us. But I will aggravate[15] my voice so that I will roar you[16] as gently as any sucking dove.[17] I will roar you an 'twere[18] any nightingale.

80   **QUINCE.** You can play no part but Pyramus, for Pyramus is a sweet-faced man, a proper man[19] as one shall see in a summer's day, a most lovely gentlemanlike man. Therefore you must needs play Pyramus.

85   **BOTTOM.** Well, I will undertake it. What beard were I best to play it in?

QUINCE. Why, what you will.

BOTTOM. I will discharge[20] it in either your[21] straw-color beard, your orange-tawny beard, your purple-in-
90   grain[22] beard, or your French-crown-color[23] beard, your perfit[24] yellow.

QUINCE. Some of your French crowns have no hair at

---

15. aggravate: Bottom means "moderate."
16. roar you: Roar for you.
17. sucking dove: Bottom mistakenly combines two references to innocence: the sucking lamb and the sitting dove.
18. an 'twere: As if it were.
19. a proper: As attractive a.
20. discharge: Play the part.
21. your: You know what I mean.
22. purple-in-grain: Dyed a colorfast dark purple.
23. French-crown-color: Gold, like a French coin.
24. perfit: Perfect, possibly spelled this way as Bottom's error.

95 all,[25] and then you will play barefaced. But, masters, here are your parts, *(giving out the parts,)* and I am to entreat you, request you, and desire you, to con[26] them by tomorrow night and meet me in the palace wood, a mile without the town, by moonlight. There will we rehearse, for if we meet in the city, we shall be dogged with company and our devices[27] known. In the meantime I will draw a bill of properties[28] such as our play wants. I pray you fail me not.

BOTTOM. We will meet, and there we may rehearse most obscenely[29] and courageously. Take pains. Be perfit. Adieu.

QUINCE. At the Duke's Oak we meet.

BOTTOM. Enough. Hold, or cut bowstrings.[30]

They exit.

25. French . . . all: A reference to a disease called the "French disease," which sometimes caused baldness.
26. con: Study; learn; memorize.
27. devices: Plans.
28. bill of properties: List of props.
29. obscenely: Bottom may mean "seemly."
30. Hold, or cut bowstrings: Similar to "Fish or cut bait," but here alluding to archery; "keep your promise or withdraw from the play."

Act II

Scene i. *Enter a Fairy at one door and Robin Good-fellow at another.*

ROBIN.

How now, spirit? Whither wander you?

FAIRY.

Over hill, over dale,
 Thorough[1] bush, thorough brier,
Over park, over pale,[2]
5   Thorough flood, thorough fire;
I do wander everywhere,
Swifter than the moon's sphere.[3]
And I serve the Fairy Queen,
To dew her orbs[4] upon the green.
10 The cowslips tall her pensioners be;[5]
In their gold coats spots you see;
Those be rubies, fairy favors;[6]
In those freckles live their savors.[7]
I must go seek some dewdrops here
15 And hang a pearl in every cowslip's ear.
Farewell, thou lob[8] of spirits. I'll be gone.
Our queen and all her elves come here anon.[9]

ROBIN.

The King doth keep his revels here tonight.
Take heed the Queen come not within his sight,
20 For Oberon is passing fell and wrath[10]
Because that she, as her attendant, hath

1. **Thorough:** Through.
2. **pale:** Enclosed park or land.
3. **moon's sphere:** According to Ptolomeic astronomy, the moon's orbit within a hollow sphere surrounding the Earth.
4. **orbs:** Rings of darker grass, also known as fairy rings.
5. **The cowslips ... pensioners be:** The flowers are compared to Queen Elizabeth's pensioners, or bodyguards, who dressed in bright colors.
6. **favors:** Gifts of love.
7. **savors:** Pleasant scents.
8. **lob:** Country oaf.
9. **anon:** Soon.
10. **passing fell and wrath:** Extremely angry; very fierce.

A lovely boy stolen from an Indian king;
She never had so sweet a changeling.[11]
And jealous Oberon would have the child
25   Knight of his train, to trace[12] the forests wild.
But she perforce[13] withholds the lovèd boy,
Crowns him with flowers, and makes him all her
    joy.
And now they never meet in grove or green,
30   By fountain[14] clear, or spangled starlight sheen,[15]
But they do square, that all[16] their elves for fear
Creep into acorn cups and hide them there.

FAIRY.

Either I mistake your shape and making quite,
Or else you are that shrewd and knavish sprite[17]
35   Called Robin Goodfellow. Are not you he
That frights the maidens of the villagery,[18]
Skim milk, and sometimes labor in the quern[19]
And bootless make the breathless huswife churn,[20]
And sometime make the drink to bear no barm,[21]
40   Mislead night wanderers, laughing at their harm?
Those that "Hobgoblin" call you, and "sweet Puck,"
You do their work, and they shall have good luck.
Are not you he?

ROBIN.   Thou speakest aright.
45   I am that merry wanderer of the night.
I jest to Oberon and make him smile
When I a fat and bean-fed horse beguile,
Neighing in likeness of a filly foal,
And sometime lurk I in a gossip's[22] bowl

---

11. changling: Child swapped for another by fairies.
12. trace: Crisscross.
13. perforce: With force.
14. fountain: Natural spring of water.
15. starlight sheen: The bright light of the stars.
16. square, that all: Fight, so that.
17. shrewd and knavish sprite: Malicious, mischevious spirit.
18. villagery: Village community.
19. quern: Small mill for grinding corn.
20. bootless . . . churn: Make all her churning useless.
21. barm: Yeasty froth on top of beer.
22. gossip's: Old woman's.

50 In very likeness of a roasted crab,[23]
And, when she drinks, against her lips I bob
And on her withered dewlap[24] pour the ale.
The wisest aunt,[25] telling the saddest tale,[26]
Sometime for three-foot stool mistaketh me;
55 Then slip I from her bum, down topples she,
And "Tailor!"[27] cries, and falls into a cough,
And then the whole choir[28] hold their hips and
    loffe[29]
And waxen[30] in their mirth and neeze[31] and swear
60 A merrier hour was never wasted there.
But room,[32] fairy. Here comes Oberon.

FAIRY.
And here my mistress. Would that he were gone!

*Enter Oberon the King of Fairies at one door, with his
train, and Titania the Queen at another, with hers.*

OBERON.
Ill met by moonlight, proud Titania.

TITANIA.
What, jealous Oberon? Fairies, skip hence.
65 I have forsworn his bed and company.

OBERON.
Tarry, rash wanton.[33] Am not I thy lord?

TITANIA.
Then I must be thy lady. But I know
When thou hast stolen away from Fairyland

---

23. crab: A kind of apple.
24. dewlap: Extra skin, lying in folds at the neck.
25. aunt: Any old woman.
26. saddest tale: Most serious or solemn story.
27. "Tailor": Many interpretations exist for this exclamation: *Tail* means "buttocks," so *tailor* could mean "O, my rear"; she ends up sitting cross-legged like a *"tailor"*; the Middle English word *taillard* means "thief."
28. choir: Assembled group.
29. loffe: Laugh.
30. waxen: Increase.
31. neeze: Sneeze.
32. room: Make room; move over.
33. rash wanton: Foolish and willful creature.

And in the shape of Corin[34] sat all day
70 Playing on pipes of corn[36] and versing love
To amorous Phillida.[35] Why art thou here,
Come from the farthest steep[37] of India,
But that, forsooth, the bouncing Amazon,
Your buskined[38] mistress and your warrior love,
75 To Theseus must be wedded, and you come
To give their bed joy and prosperity?

OBERON.

How canst thou thus for shame, Titania,
Glance at my credit[39] with Hippolyta,
Knowing I know thy love to Theseus?
80 Didst not thou lead him through the glimmering
     night
From Perigouna,[40] whom he ravishèd,
And make him with fair Aegles[41] break his faith,
With Ariadne and Antiopa?[42]

TITANIA.

85 These are the forgeries of jealousy;
And never, since the middle summer's spring,[43]
Met we on hill, in dale, forest, or mead,
By pavèd[44] fountain or by rushy brook,
Or in the beachèd margent[45] of the sea,
90 To dance our ringlets to the whistling wind,
But with thy brawls thou hast disturbed our sport.
Therefore the winds, piping to us in vain,
As in revenge have sucked up from the sea
Contagious[46] fogs, which, falling in the land,
95 Hath every pelting[47] river made so proud

34, 35. Corin; Phillida: Two traditional lovers from pastoral verse.
36. pipes of corn: Musical instrument, actually made from wheat stalks.
37. steep: Mountain, or possibly distant place.
38. buskined: Wearing buskins, a kind of boot.
39. Glance at my credit: Question my relationship with.
40, 41, 42. Perigouna; Aegles; Ariadne; Antiopa: Women Theseus is said to have loved and abandoned.
43. middle summer's spring: Beginning of midsummer.
44. pavèd: Pebbled.
45. margent: Shore.
46. Contagious: Toxic; poisonous.
47. pelting: Insignificant; petty.

That they have overborne their continents.[48]
The ox hath therefore stretched his yoke in vain,
The plowman lost his sweat, and the green corn[49]
Hath rotted ere his youth attained a beard.
100   The fold[50] stands empty in the drownèd field,
And crows are fatted with the murrain flock.[51]
The nine-men's-morris[52] is filled up with mud,
And the quaint mazes[53] in the wanton[54] green,
For lack of tread, are undistinguishable.
105   The human mortals want[55] their winter[56] here.
No night is now with hymn or carol blessed.
Therefore[57] the moon, the governess of floods,
Pale in her anger, washes all the air,
That rheumatic diseases[58] do abound.
110   And thorough this distemperature[59] we see
The seasons alter: hoary-headed frosts
Fall in the fresh lap of the crimson rose,
And on old Hiem's[60] thin and icy crown
An odorous chaplet[61] of sweet summer buds
115   Is, as in mockery, set. The spring, the summer,
The childing[62] autumn, angry winter, change
Their wonted liveries,[63] and the mazèd[64] world
By their increase now knows not which is which.
And this same progeny of evils comes

48. **continents:** Shores; banks.
49. **corn:** Here meaning any grain.
50. **fold:** Pen or corral for the sheep and cattle.
51. **murrain flock:** Herd of cattle dead from murrain, a cattle disease.
52. **nine-men's-morris:** Public space in a village in which the ground is laid out for a game of the same name.
53. **quaint mazes:** Interconnecting, and perhaps confusing, paths cut into the village green.
54. **wanton:** Thick; tall; uncut.
55. **want:** Lack.
56. **winter:** The season, or perhaps its rituals.
57. **Therefore:** Because of our argument.
58. **rheumatic diseases:** A cold, the flu, etc.
59. **distemperature:** Unsettled weather; bad moods.
60. **Hiem's:** Belonging to the winter god, Hiem.
61. **chaplet:** Wreath.
62. **childing:** Creating children; i.e., fruitful.
63. **wonted liveries:** Usual clothing or appearance.
64. **mazèd:** Confused; bewildered.

120   From our debate, from our dissension;
      We are their parents and original.[65]

OBERON.
      Do you amend it, then. It lies in you.
      Why should Titania cross her Oberon?
      I do but beg a little changeling boy
125   To be my henchman.[66]

TITANIA.   Set your heart at rest:
      The Fairyland buys not the child of me.
      His mother was a vot'ress[67] of my order,
      And in the spicèd Indian air by night
130   Full often hath she gossiped by my side
      And sat with me on Neptune's[68] yellow sands,
      Marking th' embarkèd traders on the flood,[69]
      When we have laughed to see the sails conceive
      And grow big-bellied with the wanton[70] wind;
135   Which she, with pretty and with swimming gait,
      Following her womb then rich with my young
         squire,
      Would imitate and sail upon the land
      To fetch me trifles and return again,
140   As from a voyage, rich with merchandise.
      But she, being mortal, of that boy did die,
      And for her sake do I rear up her boy,
      And for her sake I will not part with him.

OBERON.
      How long within this wood intend you stay?

TITANIA.
145   Perchance till after Theseus' wedding day.
      If you will patiently dance in our round[71]
      And see our moonlight revels, go with us.
      If not, shun me, and I will spare[72] your haunts.

65. original: Origin.
66. henchman: Attendant.
67. vot'ress: A woman sworn to serve Titania.
68. Neptune's: Belonging to the sea god, Neptune.
69. Marking . . . the flood: Noting the merchant ships at sail on the sea.
70. wanton: Unpredictable; playful.
71. round: A circular dance.
72. spare: Avoid.

OBERON.

Give me that boy and I will go with thee.

TITANIA.

150   Not for thy fairy kingdom. Fairies, away.
We shall chide downright if I longer stay.

Titania and her fairies exit.

OBERON.

Well, go thy way. Thou shalt not from[73] this grove
Till I torment thee for this injury.—
My gentle Puck, come hither. Thou rememb'rest
155   Since[74] once I sat upon a promontory
And heard a mermaid on a dolphin's back
Uttering such dulcet and harmonious breath
That the rude sea grew civil at her song
And certain stars shot madly from their spheres
160   To hear the sea-maid's music.

ROBIN.   I remember.

OBERON.

That very time I saw but thou couldst not,
Flying between the cold moon and the earth,
Cupid all armed. A certain aim he took
165   At a fair vestal[75] thronèd by the west,
And loosed his love-shaft smartly from his bow
As[76] it should pierce a hundred thousand hearts.
But I might[77] see young Cupid's fiery shaft
Quenched in the chaste beams of the wat'ry moon,
170   And the imperial vot'ress passèd on
In maiden meditation, fancy-free.[78]
Yet marked I where the bolt[79] of Cupid fell.
It fell upon a little western flower,
Before, milk-white, now purple with love's wound,

---

73. from: Go from.
74. Since: When.
75. vestal: Probably a reference to Queen Elizabeth, who remained unmarried.
76. As: As if.
77. might: Could.
78. fancy-free: Freed of love's effect.
79. bolt: Arrow.

175 And maidens call it "love-in-idleness."[80]
Fetch me that flower; the herb I showed thee once.
The juice of it on sleeping eyelids laid
Will make or man or[81] woman madly dote
Upon the next live creature that it sees.
180 Fetch me this herb, and be thou here again
Ere the leviathan[82] can swim a league.

ROBIN.
I'll put a girdle round about the earth
In forty minutes.   *(He exits.)*

OBERON.   Having once this juice,
185 I'll watch Titania when she is asleep
And drop the liquor of it in her eyes.
The next thing then she, waking, looks upon
Be it on lion, bear, or wolf, or bull,
On meddling monkey, or on busy ape
190 She shall pursue it with the soul of love.
And ere I take this charm from off her sight
As I can take it with another herb,
I'll make her render up her page to me.
But who comes here? I am invisible,
195 And I will overhear their conference.

Enter Demetrius, Helena following him.

DEMETRIUS.
I love thee not; therefore pursue me not.
Where is Lysander and fair Hermia?
The one I'll stay; the other stayeth me.
Thou told'st me they were stol'n unto this wood,
200 And here am I, and wood[83] within this wood
Because I cannot meet my Hermia.
Hence, get thee gone, and follow me no more.

HELENA.
You draw me, you hard-hearted adamant![84]
But yet you draw not iron, for my heart

80. **love-in-idleness:** Common name for the pansy flower.
81. **or . . . or:** Either man or.
82. **leviathan:** Biblical sea monster.
83. **wood:** Insane, but also a play on the word "wooed."
84. **adamant:** Hard-hearted like a diamond; pulling like a magnet.

205   Is true as steel. Leave you[85] your power to draw,
And I shall have no power to follow you.

DEMETRIUS.
> Do I entice you? Do I speak you fair?[86]
> Or rather do I not in plainest truth
> Tell you I do not, nor I cannot love you?

HELENA.
210   And even for that do I love you the more.
I am your spaniel, and, Demetrius,
The more you beat me I will fawn on you.
Use me but as your spaniel: spurn me, strike me,
Neglect me, lose me; only give me leave
215   Unworthy as I am to follow you.
What worser place can I beg in your love
And yet a place of high respect with me
Than to be usèd as you use your dog?

DEMETRIUS.
> Tempt not too much the hatred of my spirit,
220   For I am sick when I do look on thee.

HELENA.
> And I am sick when I look not on you.

DEMETRIUS.
> You do impeach[87] your modesty too much
> To leave the city and commit yourself
> Into the hands of one that loves you not,
225   To trust the opportunity of night
> And the ill counsel of a desert[88] place
> With the rich worth of your virginity.

HELENA.
> Your virtue is my privilege.[89] For that[90]
> It is not night when I do see your face,
230   Therefore I think I am not in the night.

---

85. Leave you: Give up.
86. speak you fair: Speak to you politely.
87. impeach: Question.
88. desert: Empty; deserted.
89. Your virtue . . . privilege: Your goodness is my security.
90. For that: Because.

Nor doth this wood lack worlds of company,
For you, in my respect,[91] are all the world.
Then, how can it be said I am alone
When all the world is here to look on me?

DEMETRIUS.

235   I'll run from thee and hide me in the brakes[92]
And leave thee to the mercy of wild beasts.

HELENA.

The wildest hath not such a heart as you.
Run when you will. The story shall be changed:
Apollo flies and Daphne holds the chase;[93]
240   The dove pursues the griffin; the mild hind[94]
Makes speed to catch the tiger. Bootless[95] speed
When cowardice pursues and valor flies!

DEMETRIUS.

I will not stay[96] thy questions. Let me go ,
Or if thou follow me, do not believe
245   But I shall do thee mischief in the wood.

HELENA.

Ay, in the temple, in the town, the field,
You do me mischief. Fie, Demetrius!
Your wrongs do set a scandal on my sex.[97]
We cannot fight for love as men may do.
250   We should be wooed and were not made to woo.

Demetrius exits.

I'll follow thee and make a heaven of hell
To die upon[98] the hand I love so well. *(Helena exits.)*

---

91. in my respect: In my view.
92. brakes: Bushes; thickets.
93. Apollo flies . . . the chase: Usually Apollo chases Daphne. This example, like the other two following, reverse that order so that the weaker, more chaste member of the pair pursues the stronger member.
94. hind: Doe, a female deer.
95. bootless: Ineffective; useless.
96. stay: Remain for.
97. on my sex: All women.
98. upon: At; by.

OBERON.
>Fare thee well, nymph. Ere he do leave this grove,
>Thou shalt fly him, and he shall seek thy love.

Enter Robin.

255. Hast thou the flower there? Welcome, wanderer.

ROBIN.
>Ay, there it is.

OBERON.   I pray thee give it me.

Robin gives him the flower.

>I know a bank where the wild thyme blows,[99]
>Where oxlips[100] and the nodding violet grows,
260 Quite overcanopied with luscious woodbine,[101]
>With sweet muskroses, and with eglantine.[102]
>There sleeps Titania sometime of the night,
>Lulled in these flowers with dances and delight.
>And there the snake throws[103] her enameled skin,
265 Weed[104] wide enough to wrap a fairy in.
>And with the juice of this I'll streak her eyes
>And make her full of hateful fantasies.
>Take thou some of it, and seek through this grove.

He gives Robin part of the flower.

>A sweet Athenian lady is in love
270 With a disdainful youth. Anoint his eyes,
>But do it when the next thing he espies
>May be the lady. Thou shalt know the man
>By the Athenian garments he hath on.
>Effect it with some care, that he may prove
275 More fond on[105] her than she upon her love.
>And look thou meet me ere the first cock crow.

99. blows: Blossoms.
100. oxlips: A flower like a primrose or cowslip.
101. woodbine: Honeysuckle.
102. eglantine: A kind of rose.
103. throws: Sheds; casts off.
104. Weed: Garment.
105. fond on: In love with, perhaps excessively so.

ROBIN.
Fear not, my lord; your servant shall do so.

They exit.

Scene ii. *Enter Titania, Queen of Fairies, with her train.*

TITANIA.
Come, now a roundel[1] and a fairy song;
Then, for the third part of a minute, hence—
280 Some to kill cankers[2] in the muskrose buds,
Some war with reremice[3] for their leathern wings
To make my small elves coats, and some keep back
The clamorous owl that nightly hoots and wonders
At our quaint[4] spirits. Sing me now asleep.
285 Then to your offices and let me rest. *(She lies down.)*

Fairies sing.

FIRST FAIRY.
You spotted snakes with double[5] tongue,
Thorny hedgehogs, be not seen.
Newts and blindworms,[6] do no wrong,
Come not near our Fairy Queen.

CHORUS.
290 *Philomel,[7] with melody*
Sing in our sweet lullaby.
Lulla, lulla, lullaby, lulla, lulla, lullaby.
Never harm
Nor spell nor charm
Come our lovely lady nigh.
295 *So good night, with lullaby.*

1. roundel: Dance in a circle.
2. cankers: A kind of worm.
3. reremice: Bats.
4. quaint: Delicate; dainty.
5. *double:* Split, like a fork.
6. *Newts and blindworms:* Salamanders and small snakes, once believed to be poisonous.
7. *Philomel:* Refers to a classical myth in which the king's daughter was turned into a nightingale.

FIRST FAIRY.
> *Weaving spiders, come not here.*
> > *Hence, you long-legged spinners, hence.*
> *Beetles black, approach not near.*

300
> > *Worm nor snail, do no offence.*

CHORUS.
> > *Philomel, with melody*
> > *Sing in our sweet lullaby.*
> *Lulla, lulla, lullaby, lulla, lulla, lullaby.*
> *Never harm*

305
> > *Nor spell nor charm*
> *Come our lovely lady nigh.*
> *So good night, with lullaby.*

> > *Titania sleeps.*

SECOND FAIRY.
> Hence, away! Now all is well.
> One aloof stand sentinel. *(Fairies exit.)*

Enter Oberon, who anoints Titania's eyelids with the nectar.

OBERON.

310
> > What thou seest when thou dost wake,
> > Do it for thy true love take.
> > Love and languish for his sake.
> > Be it ounce,[8] or cat, or bear,
> > Pard,[9] or boar with bristled hair,

315
> > In thy eye that shall appear
> > When thou wak'st, it is thy dear.
> > Wake when some vile thing is near. *(He exits.)*

> > *Enter Lysander and Hermia.*

LYSANDER.
> Fair love, you faint with wand'ring in the wood.
> And, to speak troth,[10] I have forgot our way.

320
> We'll rest us, Hermia, if you think it good,
> And tarry for the comfort of the day.

---

8. ounce: Lynx.
9. Pard: Leopard.
10. troth: Truth.

HERMIA.

    Be it so, Lysander. Find you out a bed,
    For I upon this bank will rest my head.

LYSANDER.

    One turf shall serve as pillow for us both;
325   One heart, one bed, two bosoms, and one troth.[11]

HERMIA.

    Nay, good Lysander. For my sake, my dear,
    Lie further off yet. Do not lie so near.

LYSANDER.

    O, take the sense, sweet, of my innocence![12]
    Love takes the meaning in love's conference.[13]
330   I mean that my heart unto yours is knit,
    So that but one heart we can make of it;
    Two bosoms interchainèd with an oath—
    So then two bosoms and a single troth.
    Then by your side no bed-room me deny,
335   For lying so, Hermia, I do not lie.

HERMIA.

    Lysander riddles very prettily.
    Now much beshrew[14] my manners and my pride
    If Hermia meant to say Lysander lied.
    But, gentle friend, for love and courtesy,
340   Lie further off in human[15] modesty.
    Such separation, as may well be said,
    Becomes a virtuous bachelor and a maid.
    So far be distant; and good night, sweet friend.
    Thy love ne'er alter till thy sweet life end!

LYSANDER.

345   "Amen, amen" to that fair prayer, say I,
    And then end life when I end loyalty!
    Here is my bed. Sleep give thee all his rest!

---

11. troth: Vow of love and faithfulness.
12. O, take . . . innocence: Grasp my true and innocent meaning.
13. Love . . . conference: Love teaches lovers to hear one another in a loving way.
14. beshrew: Mildly curse.
15. human: Civil; respectful.

HERMIA.
>With half that wish the wisher's eyes be pressed!

They sleep.

Enter Robin.

ROBIN.
>Through the forest have I gone,
350 >But Athenian found I none
>On whose eyes I might approve[16]
>This flower's force in stirring love.

He sees Lysander.

>Night and silence! Who is here?
>Weeds[17] of Athens he doth wear.
355 >This is he my master said
>Despisèd the Athenian maid.
>And here the maiden, sleeping sound
>On the dank and dirty ground.
>Pretty soul, she durst not lie
360 >Near this lack-love, this kill-courtesy.—
>Churl, upon thy eyes I throw
>All the power this charm doth owe.[18]

*He anoints Lysander's eyelids
with the nectar.*

>When thou wak'st, let love forbid
>Sleep his seat on thy eyelid.
365 >So, awake when I am gone,
>For I must now to Oberon.   *(He exits.)*

Enter Demetrius and Helena, running.

HELENA.
>Stay, though thou kill me, sweet Demetrius.

DEMETRIUS.
>I charge thee, hence, and do not haunt me thus.

16. **approve:** Try; test.
17. **Weeds:** Clothing; garments.
18. **owe:** Own; possess.

HELENA.
> O, wilt thou darkling[19] leave me? Do not so.

DEMETRIUS.
370   Stay, on thy peril. I alone will go.   *(Demetrius exits.)*

HELENA.
> O, I am out of breath in this fond[20] chase.
> The more my prayer, the lesser is my grace.[21]
> Happy is Hermia, wheresoe'er she lies,
> For she hath blessèd and attractive eyes.
375   How came her eyes so bright? Not with salt tears.
> If so, my eyes are oftener washed than hers.
> No, no, I am as ugly as a bear,
> For beasts that meet me run away for fear.
> Therefore no marvel though Demetrius
380   Do as a monster fly my presence thus.
> What wicked and dissembling glass of mine
> Made me compare with Hermia's sphery eyne?[22]
> But who is here? Lysander, on the ground!
> Dead or asleep? I see no blood, no wound.—
385   Lysander, if you live, good sir, awake.

LYSANDER. *(waking up)*
> And run through fire I will for thy sweet sake.
> Transparent[23] Helena! Nature shows art,
> That through thy bosom makes me see thy heart.
> Where is Demetrius? O, how fit a word
390   Is that vile name to perish on my sword!

HELENA.
> Do not say so. Lysander, say not so.
> What though he love your Hermia? Lord, what
>   though?
> Yet Hermia still loves you. Then be content.

LYSANDER.
395   Content with Hermia? No, I do repent
> The tedious minutes I with her have spent.

19. **darkling:** In the dark.
20. **fond:** Infatuated; foolish.
21. **grace:** Reward from prayer.
22. **compare . . . eyne:** Rival or compete with Hermia's starlike eyes.
23. **Transparent:** Able to be seen through; bright.

Not Hermia, but Helena I love.
Who will not change a raven for a dove?
The will[24] of man is by his reason swayed,
400 And reason says you are the worthier maid.
Things growing are not ripe until their season;
So I, being young, till now ripe not[25] to reason.
And touching[26] now the point of human skill,
Reason becomes the marshal to my will
405 And leads me to your eyes, where I o'erlook[27]
Love's stories written in love's richest book.

HELENA.
Wherefore[28] was I to this keen mockery born?
When at your hands did I deserve this scorn?
Is 't not enough, is 't not enough, young man,
410 That I did never, no, nor never can
Deserve a sweet look from Demetrius' eye,
But you must flout my insufficiency?
Good troth, you do me wrong, good sooth,[29] you do,
In such disdainful manner me to woo.
415 But fare you well. Perforce I must confess
I thought you lord of more true gentleness.[30]
O, that a lady of one man refused
Should of another therefore be abused! *(She exits.)*

LYSANDER.
She sees not Hermia.—Hermia, sleep thou there,
420 And never mayst thou come Lysander near.
For, as a surfeit of the sweetest things
The deepest loathing to the stomach brings,
Or as the heresies that men do leave
Are hated most of those they did deceive,[31]
425 So thou, my surfeit and my heresy,
Of all be hated, but the most of me!

24. **will:** Desire; goal.
25. **ripe not:** Have not ripened.
26. **touching . . . skill:** Attaining the limit of human judgment.
27. **o'erlook:** Scan; read.
28. **Wherefore:** Why.
29. **Good troth; good sooth:** Mild oaths that literally mean "indeed."
30. **gentleness:** Of gentle, or noble, character.
31. **of those . . . deceive:** By those whom the heresies deceived.

And, all my powers, address[32] your love and might
To honor Helen and to be her knight.   *(He exits.)*

HERMIA. *(waking up)*

Help me, Lysander, help me! Do thy best

430 To pluck this crawling serpent from my breast.
Ay me, for pity! What a dream was here!
Lysander, look how I do quake with fear.
Methought a serpent ate my heart away,
And you sat smiling at his cruel prey.[33]

435 Lysander! What, removed? Lysander, lord!
What, out of hearing? Gone? No sound, no word?
Alack, where are you? Speak, an if[34] you hear.
Speak, of all loves! I swoon almost with fear.—
No? Then I well perceive you are not nigh.

440 Either death or you I'll find immediately.

She exits.

32. **address:** Direct.
33. **prey:** To attack.
34. **an if:** If.

Act III

Scene i. With Titania still asleep onstage, enter the Clowns, Bottom, Quince, Snout, Starveling, Snug, and Flute.

BOTTOM. Are we all met?

QUINCE. Pat,[1] pat. And here's a marvels convenient place for our rehearsal. This green plot shall be our stage, this hawthorn brake[2] our tiring-house,[3] and
5   we will do it in action as we will do it before the Duke.

BOTTOM. Peter Quince?

QUINCE. What sayest thou, bully[4] Bottom?

BOTTOM. There are things in this comedy of Pyramus
10   and Thisbe that will never please. First, Pyramus must draw a sword to kill himself, which the ladies cannot abide. How answer you that?

SNOUT. By 'r lakin,[5] a parlous fear.

STARVELING. I believe we must leave the killing out,
15   when all is done.[6]

BOTTOM. Not a whit! I have a device to make all well. Write me a prologue, and let the prologue seem to say we will do no harm with our swords, and that Pyramus is not killed indeed. And, for the more
20   better assurance, tell them that I, Pyramus, am not Pyramus, but Bottom the weaver. This will put them out of fear.

---

1. Pat: Exactly; right on time.
2. brake: Thicket.
3. tiring house: Room used for dressing, or at*tiring*.
4. bully: Jolly fellow.
5. By 'r lakin: Shortened version of "By your ladykin (little lady)."
6. when all is done: After all.

QUINCE. Well, we will have such a prologue, and it shall be written in eight and six.[7]

25 **BOTTOM.** No, make it two more. Let it be written in eight and eight.

SNOUT. Will not the ladies be afeard of the lion?

STARVELING. I fear it, I promise you.

BOTTOM. Masters, you ought to consider with yourself,
30 to bring in God shield us! a lion among ladies is a most dreadful thing. For there is not a more fearful wildfowl than your lion living, and we ought to look to 't.

SNOUT. Therefore another prologue must tell he is not a
35 lion.

BOTTOM. Nay, you must name his name, and half his face must be seen through the lion's neck, and he himself must speak through, saying thus, or to the same defect: "Ladies," or "Fair ladies, I would wish
40 you," or "I would request you," or "I would entreat you not to fear, not to tremble! My life for yours. If you think I come hither as a lion, it were pity of my life.[8] No, I am no such thing. I am a man as other men are." And there indeed let him name his name
45 and tell them plainly he is Snug the joiner.

QUINCE. Well, it shall be so. But there is two hard things: that is, to bring the moonlight into a chamber, for you know Pyramus and Thisbe meet by moonlight.

50 **SNOUT.** Doth the moon shine that night we play our play?

BOTTOM. A calendar, a calendar! Look in the almanac. Find out moonshine, find out moonshine.

Quince takes out a book.

---

7. eight and six: Ballad meter containing alternating eight- and six- syllable lines.
8. it were . . . my life: Risky for me.

QUINCE. Yes, it doth shine that night.

55 **BOTTOM.** Why, then, may you leave a casement of the great chamber window, where we play, open, and the moon may shine in at the casement.

QUINCE. Ay, or else one must come in with a bush of thorns[9] and a lantern and say he comes to disfig-
60 ure[10] or to present the person of Moonshine. Then there is another thing: we must have a wall in the great chamber, for Pyramus and Thisbe, says the story, did talk through the chink of a wall.

SNOUT. You can never bring in a wall. What say you,
65 Bottom?

BOTTOM. Some man or other must present Wall. And let him have some plaster, or some loam, or some roughcast[11] about him to signify wall, or let him hold his fingers thus, and through that cranny
70 shall Pyramus and Thisbe whisper.

QUINCE. If that may be, then all is well. Come, sit down, every mother's son, and rehearse your parts. Pyramus, you begin. When you have spoken your speech, enter into that brake, and so everyone ac-
75 cording to his cue.

Enter Robin invisible to those onstage.

ROBIN. *(aside)*
What hempen homespuns[12] have we swagg'ring here
So near the cradle[13] of the Fairy Queen?
What, a play toward?[14] I'll be an auditor—
80 An actor too perhaps, if I see cause.

---

9. a bush of thorns: According to legend, the man in the moon collected firewood on Sundays and was thus banished to the sky.
10. disfigure: Bottom means *figure,* as in "symbolize" or "stand for."
11. plaster ... roughcast: Three different blended materials, each used for plastering walls.
12. hempen homespuns: Character wearing clothing homemade from hemp, probably from the country.
13. cradle: Bower where Titania sleeps.
14. toward: Being rehearsed.

QUINCE. Speak, Pyramus.—Thisbe, stand forth.

BOTTOM. *(as Pyramus)*
    Thisbe, the flowers of odious savors sweet—

QUINCE. Odors, odors!

BOTTOM. *(as Pyramus)*
                  . . . odors savors sweet.
85   *So hath thy breath, my dearest Thisbe dear.—*
    But hark, a voice! Stay thou but here awhile,
    And by and by I will to thee appear.   *(He exits.)*

ROBIN. *(aside)*
    A stranger Pyramus than e'er played here. *(He exits.)*

FLUTE. Must I speak now?

90 **QUINCE.** Ay, marry, must you, for you must understand he goes but to see a noise that he heard and is to come again.

FLUTE. *(as Thisbe)*
    Most radiant Pyramus, most lily-white of hue,
    Of color like the red rose on triumphant[15] brier,
95   *Most brisky juvenal[16] and eke[17] most lovely Jew,[18]*
    As true as truest horse, that yet would never tire.
    I'll meet thee, Pyramus, at Ninny's tomb.[19]

QUINCE. "Ninus' tomb," man! Why, you must not speak that yet. That you answer to Pyramus. You speak
100 all your part[20] at once, cues and all.—Pyramus, enter. Your cue is past. It is "never tire."

FLUTE. O!
    (As Thisbe.) As true as truest horse, that yet would never tire.

---

15. triumphant: Splendid; magnificent.
16. juvenal: Juvenile; young person.
17. eke: Also.
18. Jew: Shortening of "jewel" or repetition of "juvenal," to complete the rhyme.
19. Ninny's tomb: Refers to Ninus, legendary founder of biblical city of Nineveh.
20. part: Script containing stage cues, which Flute is accused of missing or misreading.

Enter Robin, and Bottom as Pyramus with the ass-head.[21]

BOTTOM. *(as Pyramus)*
105   *If I were fair, fair Thisbe, I were*[22] *only thine.*

QUINCE. O monstrous! O strange! We are haunted. Pray, masters, fly, masters! Help!

Quince, Flute, Snout, Snug, and Starveling exit.

ROBIN.
I'll follow you. I'll lead you about a round,[23]
   Through bog, through bush, through brake,
110   through brier.
Sometime a horse I'll be, sometime a hound,
   A hog, a headless bear, sometime a fire.[24]
And neigh, and bark, and grunt, and roar, and
   burn,
115   Like horse, hound, hog, bear, fire, at every turn.

He exits.

BOTTOM. Why do they run away? This is a knavery of them to make me afeard.

Enter Snout.

SNOUT. O Bottom, thou art changed! What do I see on thee?

120   **BOTTOM.** What do you see? You see an ass-head of your own, do you?   *(Snout exits.)*

Enter Quince.

QUINCE. Bless thee, Bottom, bless thee! Thou art translated![25]   *(He exits.)*

BOTTOM. I see their knavery. This is to make an ass of
125   me, to fright me, if they could. But I will not stir from this place, do what they can. I will walk up

---

21. **with the ass-head**: Carrying a stage prop of an ass-head.
22. **were**: Would be.
23. **about a round**: In a roundabout, like a circle dance.
24. **fire**: Will-o'-the-wisp.
25. **translated**: Changed; transformed.

and down here, and I will sing, that they shall hear
I am not afraid.

130
(He sings.) The ouzel cock,[26] so black of hue,
With orange-tawny bill,
The throstle[27] with his note so true,
The wren with little quill—[28]

TITANIA. *(waking up)*
What angel wakes me from my flow'ry bed?

BOTTOM. *(sings)*
The finch, the sparrow, and the lark,
135
The plainsong cuckoo[29] gray,
Whose note full many a man doth mark
And dares not answer "nay"—[30]
for, indeed, who would set his wit to so foolish a
bird? Who would give a bird the lie[31] though he cry
140
"cuckoo" never so?[32]

TITANIA.
I pray thee, gentle mortal, sing again.
Mine ear is much enamored of thy note,
So is mine eye enthrallèd to thy shape,
And thy fair virtue's force perforce doth move me[33]
145
On the first view to say, to swear, I love thee.

BOTTOM. Methinks, mistress, you should have little
reason for that. And yet, to say the truth, reason
and love keep little company together nowadays.
The more the pity that some honest neighbors will
150
not make them friends. Nay, I can gleek[34] upon
occasion.

26. *ouzel cock*: Male blackbird.
27. *throstle*: Thrush; a bird.
28. *quill*: Literally, a small reed pipe, but here meaning a tiny piping song.
29. *plainsong cuckoo*: Bird whose simple song is likened to church music called plainsong.
30. *Whose . . . "nay"*: Whose song married men listen to as a sign that their wives may be unfaithful, and who cannot deny that this may be so.
31. Who would . . . the lie: Who would use his intelligence to answer a foolish bird, yet who would dare to contradict the cuckoo's taunt.
32. never so: Over and over; ever so much.
33. thy . . . move me: Your beauty is so powerful it moves me whether I want it to or not.
34. gleek: Jest; joke.

TITANIA.
Thou art as wise as thou art beautiful.

BOTTOM. Not so neither; but if I had wit enough to get
out of this wood, I have enough to serve mine own
155   turn.

TITANIA.
Out of this wood do not desire to go.
Thou shalt remain here whether thou wilt or no.
I am a spirit of no common rate.[35]
The summer still doth tend[36] upon my state,
160   And I do love thee. Therefore go with me.
I'll give thee fairies to attend on thee,
And they shall fetch thee jewels from the deep
And sing while thou on pressèd flowers dost sleep.
And I will purge thy mortal grossness[37] so
165   That thou shalt like an airy spirit go.—
Peaseblossom, Cobweb, Mote,[38] and Mustardseed!

*Enter four Fairies: Peaseblossom, Cobweb,
Mote, and Mustardseed.*

PEASEBLOSSOM. Ready.

COBWEB. And I.

MOTE. And I.

170   **MUSTARDSEED.** And I.

ALL. Where shall we go?

TITANIA.
Be kind and courteous to this gentleman.
Hop in his walks and gambol in his eyes;
Feed him with apricocks and dewberries,[39]
175   With purple grapes, green figs, and mulberries;
The honey-bags steal from the humble-bees,
And for night-tapers crop their waxen thighs
And light them at the fiery glowworms' eyes

35. rate: Value; rank.
36. still doth tend: Still serves.
37. mortal grossness: The physical, mortal state of human beings.
38. Mote: A speck, but also moth, as this word was pronounced similarly.
39. apricocks and dewberries: Apricots and blackberries.

To have my love to bed and to arise;
180 And pluck the wings from painted butterflies
To fan the moonbeams from his sleeping eyes.
Nod to him, elves, and do him courtesies.

PEASEBLOSSOM. Hail, mortal!

COBWEB. Hail!

185 **MOTE.** Hail!

MUSTARDSEED. Hail!

BOTTOM. I cry your Worships mercy,[40] heartily.— I beseech your Worship's name.

COBWEB. Cobweb.

190 **BOTTOM.** I shall desire you of more acquaintance, good
Master Cobweb. If I cut my finger, I shall make
bold with you.[41]—Your name, honest gentleman?

PEASEBLOSSOM. Peaseblossom.

BOTTOM. I pray you, commend me to Mistress
195 Squash,[42] your mother, and to Master Peascod,[43]
your father. Good Master Peaseblossom, I shall desire you of more acquaintance, too.—Your name, I
beseech you, sir?

MUSTARDSEED. Mustardseed.

200 **BOTTOM.** Good Master Mustardseed, I know your patience[44] well. That same cowardly, giantlike ox-beef
hath devoured many a gentleman of your house. I
promise you, your kindred hath made my eyes
water ere now. I desire you of more acquaintance,
205 good Master Mustardseed.

TITANIA.
Come, wait upon him. Lead him to my bower.
The moon, methinks, looks with a wat'ry eye,

40. **cry . . . mercy:** Beg your pardon.
41. **Master . . . you:** Cobwebs were used to stop bleeding.
42. **Squash:** An unripe pea pod.
43. **Peascod:** A ripe pea pod.
44. **your patience:** Your story; your experiences.

And when she weeps, weeps every little flower,
Lamenting some enforcèd chastity.[45]
210   Tie up my lover's tongue. Bring him silently.

They exit.

Scene ii. *Enter Oberon, King of Fairies.*

OBERON.

I wonder if Titania be awaked;
Then what it was that next came in her eye,
Which she must dote on in extremity.[1]

Enter Robin Goodfellow.

Here comes my messenger. How now, mad spirit?
5   What night-rule[2] now about this haunted[3] grove?

ROBIN.

My mistress with a monster is in love.
Near to her close[4] and consecrated bower,
While she was in her dull[5] and sleeping hour,
A crew of patches, rude mechanicals,[6]
10   That work for bread upon Athenian stalls,
Were met together to rehearse a play
Intended for great Theseus' nuptial day.
The shallowest thick-skin of that barren sort,[7]
Who Pyramus presented in their sport,
15   Forsook his scene[8] and entered in a brake.
When I did him at this advantage take,
An ass's noll[9] I fixèd on his head.
Anon[10] his Thisbe must be answerèd,

45. **enforcèd chastity:** Violated; required.
1. **in extremity:** To the most.
2. **night-rule:** Events or mood typical of the night.
3. **haunted:** Often visited.
4. **close:** Hidden; secret.
5. **dull:** Drowsy or perhaps sleeping.
6. **patches, rude mechanicals:** Fools, uneducated workers.
7. **barren sort:** Stupid type.
8. **scene:** Stage.
9. **noll:** Short for noodle, or head.
10. **Anon:** Any minute.

And forth my mimic[11] comes. When they him spy,
20 As wild geese that the creeping fowler[12] eye,
Or russet-pated choughs, many in sort,[13]
Rising and cawing at the gun's report,
Sever[14] themselves and madly sweep the sky,
So at his sight away his fellows fly,
25 And, at our stamp, here o'er and o'er one falls.
He "Murder" cries and help from Athens calls.
Their sense thus weak, lost with their fears thus
    strong,
Made senseless things begin to do them wrong;
30 For briers and thorns at their apparel snatch,
Some sleeves, some hats, from yielders all things
    catch.[15]
I led them on in this distracted fear
And left sweet Pyramus translated there.
35 When in that moment, so it came to pass,
Titania waked and straightway loved an ass.

OBERON.

This falls out better than I could devise.
But hast thou yet latched[16] the Athenian's eyes
With the love juice, as I did bid thee do?

ROBIN.

40 I took him sleeping—that is finished, too—
And the Athenian woman by his side,
That, when he waked, of force[17] she must be eyed.

Enter Demetrius and Hermia.

OBERON.

Stand close.[18] This is the same Athenian.

---

11. **mimic:** A comic actor.
12. **fowler:** Game bird hunter.
13. **russet-pated . . . sort:** A flock of jackdaws with brownish heads.
14. **Sever:** Disperse; scatter.
15. **from . . . catch:** Those who are afraid invite attack.
16. **latched:** Caught; fastened.
17. **of force:** By need.
18. **Stand close:** Move into hiding.

ROBIN.

This is the woman, but not this the man.

They step aside.

DEMETRIUS.

45   O, why rebuke you him that loves you so?
Lay breath so bitter on your bitter foe!

HERMIA.

Now I but chide, but I should use thee worse,
For thou, I fear, hast given me cause to curse.
If thou hast slain Lysander in his sleep,
50   Being o'er shoes[19] in blood, plunge in the deep
And kill me too.
The sun was not so true unto the day
As he to me. Would he have stolen away
From sleeping Hermia? I'll believe as soon
55   This whole earth may be bored, and that the moon
May through the center creep and so displease
Her brother's noontide with th' Antipodes.[20]
It cannot be but thou hast murdered him.
So should a murderer look, so dead,[21] so grim.

DEMETRIUS.

60   So should the murdered look, and so should I,
Pierced through the heart with your stern cruelty.
Yet you, the murderer, look as bright, as clear,
As yonder Venus in her glimmering sphere.

HERMIA.

What's this to my Lysander? Where is he?
65   Ah, good Demetrius, wilt thou give him me?

DEMETRIUS.

I had rather give his carcass to my hounds.

---

19. o'er shoes: Wading in.
20. This whole . . . th' Antipodes: This figurative language describes an image
in which the "whole," or solid, globe is pierced through. The moon moves
through that tunnel to disrupt the daytime and bring night to the Antipodes, or
opposite side of the globe.
21. so dead: Pale as a dead person.

HERMIA.
>Out, dog! Out, cur! Thou driv'st me past the
> bounds
>Of maiden's patience. Hast thou slain him, then?
70 Henceforth be never numbered among men.
>O, once tell true! Tell true, even for my sake!
>Durst thou have looked upon him, being awake?
>And hast thou killed him sleeping? O brave touch![22]
>Could not a worm, an adder, do so much?
75 An adder did it, for with doubler tongue
>Than thine, thou serpent, never adder stung.

DEMETRIUS.
>You spend your passion on a misprised mood.[23]
>I am not guilty of Lysander's blood,
>Nor is he dead, for aught that I can tell.

HERMIA.
80 I pray thee, tell me then that he is well.

DEMETRIUS.
>An if I could, what should I get therefor?

HERMIA.
>A privilege never to see me more.
>And from thy hated presence part I so.
>See me no more, whether he be dead or no.

>>*She exits.*

DEMETRIUS.
85 There is no following her in this fierce vein.
>Here, therefore, for a while I will remain.
>So sorrow's heaviness doth heavier grow
>For debt that bankrout sleep doth sorrow owe,
>Which now in some slight measure it will pay,
90 If for his tender here I make some stay.[24]

>>*He lies down and falls asleep.*

22. O brave touch!: Admirable action, but meant ironically.
23. misprised mood: Anger or grief based on misunderstanding.
24. So sorrow's . . . stay: *Heavy* can be read as both "sad" and "drowsy." Demetrius, who has perhaps been unable to sleep for unhappiness, hopes to relieve his sorrow with sleep. Sleep has been *bankrupt,* or "unable to offer relief so far."

OBERON. *(to Robin)*
What hast thou done? Thou hast mistaken quite
And laid the love juice on some true-love's sight.
Of thy misprision[25] must perforce ensue
Some true-love turned, and not a false turned true.

ROBIN.
95 Then fate o'errules, that, one man holding troth,
A million fail, confounding oath on oath.[26]

OBERON.
About the wood go swifter than the wind,
And Helena of Athens look thou[27] find.
All fancy-sick[28] she is and pale of cheer[29]
100 With sighs of love that costs the fresh blood dear.[30]
By some illusion see thou bring her here.
I'll charm his eyes against[31] she do appear.

ROBIN. I go, I go, look how I go,
Swifter than arrow from the Tartar's bow.[32] *(He exits.)*

OBERON. *(applying the nectar to Demetrius' eyes)*
105 Flower of this purple dye,
Hit with Cupid's archery,
Sink in apple of his eye.
When his love he doth espy,
Let her shine as gloriously
110 As the Venus of the sky.
When thou wak'st, if she be by,
Beg of her for remedy.

Enter Robin.

ROBIN.
Captain of our fairy band,
Helena is here at hand,

25. **misprision:** Error; mistake.
26. **confounding . . . oath:** Breaking promise after promise.
27. **look thou:** Be sure you.
28. **fancy-sick:** Lovesick.
29. **cheer:** Face.
30. **sighs . . . dear:** Reference to the then-popular theory that each sigh depleted the blood.
31. **against:** To prepare for.
32. **Tartar's bow:** Tartar's were good bowsmen with strong bows.

115   And the youth, mistook by me,
        Pleading for a lover's fee.[33]
        Shall we their fond pageant[34] see?
        Lord, what fools these mortals be!

OBERON.
        Stand aside. The noise they make
120   Will cause Demetrius to awake.

ROBIN.
        Then will two at once woo one.
        That must needs be sport alone.[35]
        And those things do best please me
        That befall prepost'rously.

                    They step aside.

            Enter Lysander and Helena.

LYSANDER.
125   Why should you think that I should woo in scorn?
            Scorn and derision never come in tears.
        Look when[36] I vow, I weep; and vows so born,
            In their nativity all truth appears.
        How can these things in me seem scorn to you,
130   Bearing the badge of faith[37] to prove them true?

HELENA.
        You do advance[38] your cunning more and more.
            When truth kills truth,[39] O devilish holy fray!
        These vows are Hermia's. Will you give her o'er?
            Weigh oath with oath, and you will nothing
135   weigh.
        Your vows to her and me, put in two scales,
        Will even weigh, and both as light as tales.

LYSANDER.
        I had no judgment when to her I swore.

33. fee: Privilege.
34. fond pageant: Silly spectacle.
35. sport alone: The best entertainment.
36. Look when: While; whenever.
37. badge of faith: Lysander's tears.
38. advance: Show.
39. truth kills truth: Lysander's two vows are at odds; he cannot keep both.

HELENA.
Nor none, in my mind, now you give her o'er.

LYSANDER.
140   Demetrius loves her, and he loves not you.

DEMETRIUS. *(waking up)*
O Helen, goddess, nymph, perfect, divine!
To what, my love, shall I compare thine eyne?
Crystal is muddy. O, how ripe in show[40]
Thy lips, those kissing cherries, tempting grow!
145   That pure congealèd white, high Taurus'[41] snow,
Fanned with the eastern wind, turns to a crow
When thou hold'st up thy hand. O, let me kiss
This princess of pure white, this seal[42] of bliss!

HELENA.
O spite! O hell! I see you all are bent
150   To set against[43] me for your merriment.
If you were civil and knew courtesy,
You would not do me thus much injury.
Can you not hate me, as I know you do,
But you must join in souls to mock me too?
155   If you were men, as men you are in show,
You would not use a gentle lady so,
To vow and swear and superpraise my parts,[44]
When, I am sure, you hate me with your hearts.
You both are rivals and love Hermia,
160   And now both rivals to mock Helena.
A trim exploit, a manly enterprise,
To conjure tears up in a poor maid's eyes
With your derision! None of noble sort
Would so offend a virgin and extort[45]
165   A poor soul's patience, all to make you sport.

---

40. show: Appearance.
41. Taurus': Found in Asia's Taurus Mountains.
42. seal: Promise; pledge.
43. set against: Attack.
44. parts: Characteristics; qualities.
45. extort: Extract by wearing down as if through torture.

LYSANDER.
>You are unkind, Demetrius. Be not so,
>For you love Hermia; this you know I know.
>And here with all goodwill, with all my heart,
>In Hermia's love I yield you up my part.
170 And yours of Helena to me bequeath,
>Whom I do love and will do till my death.

HELENA.
>Never did mockers waste more idle breath.

DEMETRIUS.
>Lysander, keep thy Hermia. I will none.[46]
>If e'er I loved her, all that love is gone.
175 My heart to her but as guest-wise sojourned,[47]
>And now to Helen is it home returned,
>There to remain.

LYSANDER.   Helen, it is not so.

DEMETRIUS.
>Disparage not the faith thou dost not know,
180 Lest to thy peril thou aby it[48] dear.
>Look where thy love comes. Yonder is thy dear.

Enter Hermia.

HERMIA. *(to Lysander)*
>Dark night, that from the eye his[49] function takes,
>The ear more quick of apprehension makes;
>Wherein it doth impair the seeing sense,
185 It pays the hearing double recompense.
>Thou art not by mine eye, Lysander, found;
>Mine ear, I thank it, brought me to thy sound.
>But why unkindly didst thou leave me so?

LYSANDER.
>Why should he stay whom love doth press to go?

HERMIA.
190 What love could press Lysander from my side?

46. I will none: I will have no part of her.
47. sojourned: Stayed; visited.
48. aby it: Pay for it.
49. his: Its.

LYSANDER.

Lysander's love, that would not let him bide,
Fair Helena, who more engilds the night
Than all yon fiery oes[50] and eyes of light.
Why seek'st thou me? Could not this make thee
195   know
The hate I bear thee made me leave thee so?

HERMIA.

You speak not as you think. It cannot be.

HELENA.

Lo, she is one of this confederacy!
Now I perceive they have conjoined all three
200   To fashion this false sport in spite of me.—[51]
Injurious Hermia, most ungrateful maid,
Have you conspired, have you with these contrived,
To bait[52] me with this foul derision?
Is all the counsel that we two have shared,
205   The sisters' vows, the hours that we have spent
When we have chid the hasty-footed time
For parting us—O, is all forgot?
All schooldays' friendship, childhood innocence?
We, Hermia, like two artificial[53] gods,
210   Have with our needles created both one flower,
Both on one sampler, sitting on one cushion,
Both warbling of one song, both in one key,
As if our hands, our sides, voices, and minds
Had been incorporate.[54] So we grew together
215   Like to a double cherry, seeming parted,
But yet an union in partition,
Two lovely berries molded on one stem;
So with two seeming bodies but one heart,
Two of the first, like coats in heraldry,
220   Due but to one, and crownèd with one crest.[55]

50. oes: Round spangles, here stars.
51. in spite of me: To annoy me.
52. contrived,/To bait: Plotted to harass.
53. artificial: Skilled, as an artist would be.
54. incorporate: Joined as one body.
55. Two . . . crest: Like a shield on which the coat of arms appears twice under one crest, Helena and Hermia—despite their two bodies—share a single heart.

And will you rent[56] our ancient love asunder,
To join with men in scorning your poor friend?
It is not friendly; 'tis not maidenly.
Our sex, as well as I, may chide you for it,
225 Though I alone do feel the injury.

HERMIA.
I am amazèd at your words.
I scorn you not. It seems that you scorn me.

HELENA.
Have you not set Lysander, as in scorn,
To follow me and praise my eyes and face,
230 And made your other love, Demetrius,
Who even but now did spurn me with his foot,
To call me goddess, nymph, divine and rare,
Precious, celestial? Wherefore speaks he this
To her he hates? And wherefore doth Lysander
235 Deny your love so rich within his soul
And tender[57] me, forsooth, affection,
But by your setting on, by your consent?
What though I be not so in grace[58] as you,
So hung upon with love, so fortunate,
240 But miserable most, to love unloved?
This you should pity rather than despise.

HERMIA.
I understand not what you mean by this.

HELENA.
Ay, do. Persever,[59] counterfeit sad[60] looks,
Make mouths upon[61] me when I turn my back,
245 Wink each at other, hold the sweet jest up.
This sport, well carried,[62] shall be chronicled.
If you have any pity, grace, or manners,
You would not make me such an argument.[63]

56. **rent:** Tear (from rend).
57. **tender:** Offer.
58. **in grace:** Favored.
59. **Persever:** Persevere.
60. **sad:** Serious.
61. **Make mouths upon:** Make mocking faces at.
62. **carried:** Managed.
63. **argument:** Subject of discussion or jest.

250 But fare you well. 'Tis partly my own fault,
Which death or absence soon shall remedy.

LYSANDER.
Stay, gentle Helena. Hear my excuse,
My love, my life, my soul, fair Helena.

HELENA.
O excellent!

HERMIA. *(to Lysander)*
Sweet, do not scorn her so.

DEMETRIUS. *(to Lysander)*
255 If she cannot entreat,[64] I can compel.

LYSANDER.
Thou canst compel no more than she entreat.
Thy threats have no more strength than her weak
  prayers.—
Helen, I love thee. By my life, I do.
260 I swear by that which I will lose for thee,
To prove him false that says I love thee not.

DEMETRIUS.
I say I love thee more than he can do.

LYSANDER.
If thou say so, withdraw and prove it too.

DEMETRIUS.
Quick, come.

265 **HERMIA.**   Lysander, whereto tends all this?

She takes hold of Lysander.

LYSANDER.
Away, you Ethiop![65]

DEMETRIUS. *(to Hermia)*
    No, no. He'll

64 entreat: Persuade through pleading.
65. Ethiop: Of dark hair and skin color, through a reference to an Ethiopian or dark-skinned African.

Seem to break loose. *(To Lysander.)* Take on as[66]
    you would follow,
270 But yet come not. You are a tame man, go!

LYSANDER. *(to Hermia)*
Hang off, thou cat, thou burr! Vile thing, let loose,
Or I will shake thee from me like a serpent.

HERMIA.
Why are you grown so rude? What change is this,
Sweet love?

275 **LYSANDER.**   Thy love? Out, tawny Tartar,[67] out!
Out, loathèd med'cine! O, hated potion, hence!

HERMIA.
Do you not jest?

HELENA.   Yes, sooth,[68] and so do you.

LYSANDER.
Demetrius, I will keep my word[69] with thee.

DEMETRIUS.
280 I would I had your bond. For I perceive
A weak bond[70] holds you. I'll not trust your word.

LYSANDER.
What? Should I hurt her, strike her, kill her dead?
Although I hate her, I'll not harm her so.

HERMIA.
What, can you do me greater harm than hate?
285 Hate me? Wherefore? O me, what news,[71] my love?
Am not I Hermia? Are not you Lysander?
I am as fair now as I was erewhile.[72]
Since night you loved me; yet since night you left
    me.

66. **Take on as:** Act as if.
67. **Tartar:** Gypsy.
68. **sooth:** A mild oath meaning "truly."
69. **my word:** My challenge; my threat.
70. **bond . . . bond:** The word *bond* is used to mean both "legal contract" and "restraint," thus creating a play on words.
71. **what news:** What has happened?
72. **erewhile:** Before; just now.

290   Why, then, you left me—O, the gods forbid!—
In earnest, shall I say?

LYSANDER.   Ay, by my life,
And never did desire to see thee more.
Therefore be out of hope, of question, of doubt.
295   Be certain, nothing truer, 'tis no jest
That I do hate thee and love Helena.

Hermia turns him loose.

HERMIA.
O me! *(To Helena.)* You juggler, you cankerblossom,[73]
You thief of love! What, have you come by night
And stol'n my love's heart from him?

300 **HELENA.**   Fine, i' faith.
Have you no modesty, no maiden shame,
No touch of bashfulness? What, will you tear
Impatient answers from my gentle tongue?
Fie, fie, you counterfeit, you puppet, you!

HERMIA.
305   "Puppet"? Why so? Ay, that way goes the game.
Now I perceive that she hath made compare
Between our statures; she hath urged her height,
And with her personage, her tall personage,
Her height, forsooth, she hath prevailed with him.
310   And are you grown so high in his esteem
Because I am so dwarfish and so low?
How low am I, thou painted maypole? Speak!
How low am I? I am not yet so low
But that my nails can reach unto thine eyes.

HELENA.
315   I pray you, though you mock me, gentlemen,
Let her not hurt me. I was never curst;[74]
I have no gift at all in shrewishness.
I am a right maid[75] for my cowardice.
Let her not strike me. You perhaps may think,

73. **cankerblossom:** A worm that destroys blossoms.
74. **curst:** Shrewish (as in line 317); quarrelsome.
75. **right maid:** An essentially feminine girl, perhaps a sissy.

320   Because she is something[76] lower than myself,
       That I can match her.

HERMIA.   "Lower"? Hark, again!

HELENA.
       Good Hermia, do not be so bitter with me.
       I evermore did love you, Hermia,
325   Did ever keep your counsels, never wronged you—
       Save that, in love unto Demetrius,
       I told him of your stealth unto this wood.
       He followed you; for love, I followed him.
       But he hath chid me hence[77] and threatened me
330   To strike me, spurn me, nay, to kill me too.
       And now, so you will let me quiet go,
       To Athens will I bear my folly back
       And follow you no further. Let me go.
       You see how simple and how fond[78] I am.

HERMIA.
335   Why, get you gone. Who is 't that hinders you?

HELENA.
       A foolish heart that I leave here behind.

HERMIA.
       What, with Lysander?

HELENA.   With Demetrius.

LYSANDER.
       Be not afraid. She shall not harm thee, Helena.

DEMETRIUS.
340   No, sir, she shall not, though you take her part.

HELENA.
       O, when she is angry, she is keen and shrewd.[79]
       She was a vixen when she went to school,
       And though she be but little, she is fierce.

---

76. something: Somewhat.
77. chid me hence: Pushed me away by his scolding.
78. fond: Perhaps overfond; foolish.
79. keen and shrewd: Cruel, sharp-tongued, and shrewish.

HERMIA.

345 "Little" again? Nothing but "low" and "little"?
Why will you suffer her to flout me thus?
Let me come to her.

LYSANDER.   Get you gone, you dwarf,
You minimus[80] of hind'ring knotgrass[81] made,
You bead, you acorn—

350 **DEMETRIUS.**   You are too officious
In her behalf that scorns your services.
Let her alone. Speak not of Helena.
Take not her part. For if thou dost intend
Never so little show of love to her,
355 Thou shalt aby[82] it.

LYSANDER.   Now she holds me not.
Now follow, if thou dar'st, to try whose right,
Of thine or mine, is most in Helena.

DEMETRIUS.

"Follow"? Nay, I'll go with thee, cheek by jowl.

Demetrius and Lysander exit.

HERMIA.

360 You, mistress, all this coil is long of you.[83]

Helena retreats.

Nay, go not back.

HELENA.   I will not trust you, I,
Nor longer stay in your curst company.
Your hands than mine are quicker for a fray.
365 My legs are longer though, to run away. (*She exits.*)

HERMIA.

I am amazed[84] and know not what to say.

(*She exits.*)

---

80. minimus: Tiniest thing.
81. knotgrass: A weed believed to stunt growth.
82. aby: Pay for.
83. coil is long of you: All this upset was caused by you.
84. amazed: Confused; disoriented (as in a maze).

OBERON. *(to Robin)*
> This is thy negligence. Still thou mistak'st,
> Or else committ'st thy knaveries willfully.

ROBIN.
> Believe me, king of shadows, I mistook.
370 > Did not you tell me I should know the man
> By the Athenian garments he had on?
> And so far blameless proves my enterprise
> That I have 'nointed an Athenian's eyes;
> And so far am I glad it so did sort,[85]
375 > As[86] this their jangling I esteem a sport.

OBERON.
> Thou seest these lovers seek a place to fight.
> Hie,[87] therefore, Robin, overcast the night;
> The starry welkin[88] cover thou anon
> With drooping fog as black as Acheron,[89]
380 > And lead these testy rivals so astray
> As[90] one come not within another's way.
> Like to Lysander sometime frame thy tongue;
> Then stir Demetrius up with bitter wrong.[91]
> And sometime rail thou like Demetrius.
385 > And from each other look thou lead them thus,
> Till o'er their brows death-counterfeiting sleep
> With leaden legs and batty[92] wings doth creep.
> Then crush this herb[93] into Lysander's eye,

He gives the flower to Robin.

> Whose liquor hath this virtuous[94] property,
390 > To take from thence all error with his[95] might

85. it so did sort: It did resolve itself.
86. As: Since.
87. Hie: Hasten.
88. welkin: Sky.
89. Acheron: Hell—the reference is to Hades, one of the rivers of the underworld in classical mythology.
90. As: That.
91. wrong: Injuries; insults.
92. batty: Like a bat's.
93. herb: Plant—here, an antidote to the earlier love-in-idleness.
94. virtuous: Strong; potent.
95. his: Its.

And make his eyeballs roll with wonted sight.
When they next wake, all this derision[96]
Shall seem a dream and fruitless vision.
And back to Athens shall the lovers wend,
395   With league whose date[97] till death shall never end.
Whiles I in this affair do thee employ,
I'll to my queen and beg her Indian boy;
And then I will her charmèd eye release
From monster's view, and all things shall be peace.

ROBIN.

400   My fairy lord, this must be done with haste,
For night's swift dragons cut the clouds full fast,
And yonder shines Aurora's harbinger,[98]
At whose approach, ghosts wand'ring here and
    there
405   Troop home to churchyards. Damnèd spirits all,
That in crossways and floods have burial,[99]
Already to their wormy beds are gone.
For fear lest day should look their shames upon,
They willfully themselves exile from light
410   And must for aye[100] consort with black-browed
    night.

OBERON.

But we are spirits of another sort.
I with the Morning's love[101] have oft made sport
And, like a forester, the groves may tread
415   Even till the eastern gate, all fiery red,
Opening on Neptune with fair blessèd beams,
Turns into yellow gold his salt-green streams.
But notwithstanding, haste! Make no delay.
We may effect this business yet ere day.   *(He exits.)*

---

96. derision: Absurd, laughable situation.
97. With league whose date: Joined for a term or time.
98. Aurora's harbinger: The morning star, Venus, announces the arrival of Aurora, the dawn.
99. crossways . . . burial: A reference to those lacking proper burial—here, suicides who were buried at crossroads and flood victims who floated away.
100. for aye: For always.
101. Morning's love: Possibly Aurora herself or her lover, Cephalus.

ROBIN.
420   Up and down, up and down,
I will lead them up and down.
I am feared in field and town.
Goblin,[102] lead them up and down.
Here comes one.

Enter Lysander.

LYSANDER.
425   Where art thou, proud Demetrius? Speak thou now.

ROBIN. *(in Demetrius' voice)*
Here, villain, drawn[103] and ready. Where art thou?

LYSANDER. I will be with thee straight.[104]

ROBIN. *(in Demetrius' voice)* Follow me, then,
430   to plainer[105] ground.   *(Lysander exits.)*

Enter Demetrius.

DEMETRIUS. Lysander, speak again.
Thou runaway, thou coward, art thou fled?
Speak! In some bush? Where dost thou hide thy head?

ROBIN. *(in Lysander's voice)*
435   Thou coward, art thou bragging to the stars,
Telling the bushes that thou look'st for wars,
And wilt not come? Come, recreant![106] Come, thou child!
I'll whip thee with a rod. He is defiled
440   That draws a sword on thee.

DEMETRIUS.   Yea, art thou there?

102. **Goblin:** Literally, hobgoblin; here referring to Puck/Robin Goodfellow.
103. **drawn:** With my sword ready.
104. **straight:** Directly; immediately.
105. **plainer:** More level; flatter.
106. **recreant:** Pathetic, cowardly wretch.

ROBIN. *(in Lysander's voice)*
Follow my voice. We'll try no manhood here.[107]

They exit.

Enter Lysander.

LYSANDER.
He goes before me and still dares me on.
When I come where he calls, then he is gone.
445   The villain is much lighter-heeled than I.
I followed fast, but faster he did fly,
That fallen am I in dark uneven way,
And here will rest me. Come, thou gentle day,
For if but once thou show me thy gray light,
450   I'll find Demetrius and revenge this spite.

He lies down and sleeps.

Enter Robin and Demetrius.

ROBIN. *(in Lysander's voice)*
Ho, ho, ho! Coward, why com'st thou not?

DEMETRIUS.
Abide me,[108] if thou dar'st, for well I wot[109]
Thou runn'st before me, shifting every place,
And dar'st not stand nor look me in the face.
455   Where art thou now?

ROBIN. *(in Lysander's voice)*
                  Come hither. I am here.

DEMETRIUS.
Nay, then, thou mock'st me. Thou shalt buy this
    dear[110]
If ever I thy face by daylight see.
460   Now go thy way. Faintness constraineth me
To measure out my length on this cold bed.
By day's approach look to be visited.

He lies down and sleeps.

107. **We'll . . . here:** We won't test our bravery here.
108. **Abide me:** Confront me.
109. **wot:** Know.
110. **buy this dear:** Pay for this dearly.

Enter Helena.

HELENA.

O weary night, O long and tedious night,
  Abate[111] thy hours! Shine, comforts, from the
465   east,
That I may back to Athens by daylight
  From these that my poor company detest.
And sleep, that sometimes shuts up sorrow's eye,
Steal me awhile from mine own company.

She lies down and sleeps.

ROBIN.

470   Yet but three? Come one more.
Two of both kinds makes up four.
Here she comes, curst[112] and sad.
Cupid is a knavish lad
Thus to make poor females mad.

Enter Hermia.

HERMIA.

475   Never so weary, never so in woe,
  Bedabbled with the dew and torn with briers,
I can no further crawl, no further go.
  My legs can keep no pace with my desires.
Here will I rest me till the break of day.
480   Heavens shield Lysander if they mean a fray!

She lies down and sleeps.

ROBIN.

On the ground
Sleep sound.
I'll apply
To your eye,
485   Gentle lover, remedy.

*Robin applies the nectar
to Lysander's eyes.*

When thou wak'st,

---

111. **Abate:** Shorten.
112. **curst:** In a bad mood; angry.

Thou tak'st
True delight
In the sight
490 Of thy former lady's eye.
And the country proverb known,
That every man should take his own,
In your waking shall be shown.
Jack shall have Jill;
495 Nought shall go ill;
The man shall have his mare again, and all shall be
well.

He exits.

Act IV

*Scene i. With the four lovers still asleep onstage,
enter Titania, Queen of Fairies, and Bottom and
Fairies, and Oberon, the King, behind them unseen
by those onstage.*

TITANIA.
Come, sit thee down upon this flow'ry bed,
While I thy amiable[1] cheeks do coy,[2]
And stick muskroses in thy sleek smooth head,
And kiss thy fair large ears, my gentle joy.

5 **BOTTOM.** Where's Peaseblossom?

PEASEBLOSSOM. Ready.

BOTTOM. Scratch my head, Peaseblossom. Where's
Monsieur Cobweb?

COBWEB. Ready.

10 **BOTTOM.** Monsieur Cobweb; good monsieur, get you
your weapons in your hand and kill me a red-
hippd humble-bee on the top of a thistle, and, good
monsieur, bring me the honey-bag. Do not fret
yourself too much in the action, monsieur, and,
15 good monsieur, have a care the honey-bag break
not; I would be loath to have you overflown with a
honey-bag, signior. *(Cobweb exits.)* Where's Monsieur Mustardseed?

MUSTARDSEED. Ready.

20 **BOTTOM.** Give me your neaf,[3] Monsieur Mustardseed.
Pray you, leave your courtesy,[4] good monsieur.

MUSTARDSEED. What's your will?

1. **amiable:** Lovable.
2. **coy:** Caress.
3. **neaf:** Hand.
4. **leave your courtesy:** Stop bowing; leave your hat on.

BOTTOM. Nothing, good mounsier, but to help Cavalery[5] Cobweb[6] to scratch. I must to the barber's, monsieur, for methinks I am marvels[7] hairy about the face. And I am such a tender ass, if my hair do but tickle me, I must scratch.

TITANIA.
What, wilt thou hear some music, my sweet love?

BOTTOM. I have a reasonable good ear in music. Let's have the tongs and the bones.[8]

TITANIA.
Or say, sweet love, what thou desirest to eat.

BOTTOM. Truly, a peck of provender. I could munch your good dry oats. Methinks I have a great desire to a bottle[9] of hay. Good hay, sweet hay, hath no fellow.[10]

TITANIA.
I have a venturous fairy that shall seek
The squirrel's hoard and fetch thee new nuts.

BOTTOM. I had rather have a handful or two of dried peas. But, I pray you, let none of your people stir me; I have an exposition[11] of sleep come upon me.

TITANIA.
Sleep thou, and I will wind thee in my arms.—
Fairies, begone, and be all ways[12] away.

Fairies exit.

So doth the woodbine the sweet honeysuckle
Gently entwist; the female ivy so

---

5. **Cavalry:** Cavalier, an address for a gentleman.
6. **Cobweb:** Considered by many editors to be an error, as Cobweb is offstage at this point. Some editors believe this should be Peaseblossom.
7. **marvels:** Marvelous.
8. **tongs . . . bones:** Musical instruments common to rustic music. Tongs were similar to a triangle, while the bones were clapped together.
9. **bottle:** Bundle.
10. **fellow:** Equal.
11. **exposition:** Bottom means "disposition."
12. **be all ways:** In every direction.

45   Enrings the barky fingers of the elm.
       O, how I love thee! How I dote on thee!

                              Bottom and Titania sleep.

                       Enter Robin Goodfellow.

OBERON.
       Welcome, good Robin. Seest thou this sweet sight?
       Her dotage now I do begin to pity.
       For, meeting her of late behind the wood,
50   Seeking sweet favours[13] for this hateful fool,
       I did upbraid her and fall out with her.
       For she his hairy temples then had rounded
       With coronet of fresh and fragrant flowers;
       And that same dew, which sometime[14] on the buds
55   Was wont to swell like round and orient pearls,[15]
       Stood now within the pretty flouriets'[16] eyes,
       Like tears that did their own disgrace bewail.
       When I had at my pleasure taunted her,
       And she in mild terms beggd my patience,
60   I then did ask of her her changeling child,
       Which straight she gave me, and her fairy sent
       To bear him to my bower in Fairyland.
       And now I have the boy, I will undo
       This hateful imperfection of her eyes.
65   And, gentle Puck, take this transformèd scalp
       From off the head of this Athenian swain,
       That he, awaking when the other[17] do,
       May all to Athens back again repair,[18]
       And think no more of this night's accidents[19]
70   But as the fierce vexation of a dream.
       But first I will release the Fairy Queen.

                       He applies the nectar to her eyes.

13. favors: Gifts; here, probably flowers.
14. sometime: Formerly.
15. orient pearls: Pearls from the Orient, considered the finest.
16. flouriets: Small flowers.
17. other: Others.
18. repair: Return; travel to.
19. accidents: Events.

Be as thou wast wont to be;
See as thou was wont to see.
Dian's bud o'er Cupid's flower [20]

75　　　Hath such force and blessed power.
Now, my Titania, wake you, my sweet queen.

TITANIA. *(waking)*
My Oberon, what visions have I seen!
Methought I was enamoured of an ass.

OBERON.
There lies your love.

80　**TITANIA.**　　　　　How came these things to pass?
O, how mine eyes do loathe his visage now!

OBERON.
Silence awhile.—Robin, take off this head.—
Titania, music call; and strike more dead
Than common sleep of all these five [21] the sense.

TITANIA.
85　Music, ho, music, such as charmeth sleep!

ROBIN. *(Removing the ass-head from Bottom)*
Now, when thou wak'st with thine own fool's eyes
　　peep.

OBERON.
Sound, music.　　　　　　　　　*(Music)*
　　　　　Come, my Queen, take hands with
90　me,
And rock the ground whereon these sleepers be.

Titania and Oberon dance.

Now thou and I are new in amity,
And will tomorrow midnight solemnly [22]
Dance in Duke Thseus' house triumphantly, [23]

---

20. Dian's bud . . . flower: Here, Oberon uses a second flower as an antidote
to love-in-idleness, which he calls Cupid's flower. The antidote flower is Dian's
bud because Diana is the goddess of chastity and therefore opposite to Cupid,
the god of love.
21. all these five: Bottom plus the four lovers.
22, solemnly: With ceremony.
23. triumphantly: With festivity.

95   And bless it to all fair prosperity.
There shall the pairs of faithful lovers be
Wedded, with Theseus, an in jollity.

ROBIN.

Fairy king, attend and mark.
I do hear the morning lark.

OBERON.

100   Then, my queen, in silence sad,[24]
Trip we after night's shade.
We the globe can compass soon,
Swifter than the wand'ring moon.

TITANIA.

Come, my lord, and in our flight
105   Tell me how it came this night
That I sleeping here was found
With these mortals on the ground.

Oberon, Robin, and Titania exit.

Wind horn. Enter Theseus and all his train,
Hippolyta, Egeus.

THESEUS.

Go, one of you, find out the Forester.
For now our observation[25] is performed,
110   And, since we have the vaward[26] of the day,
My love shall hear the music of my hounds.
Uncouple[27] in the western valley; let them go.
Dispatch, I say, and find the Forester.

A Servant exits.

We will, fair queen, up to the mountain's top
115   And mark the musical confusion
Of hounds and echo in conjunction.

24. **sad:** Serious; sober.
25. **our observation:** Our ritual observing May Day.
26. **vaward:** Vanguard, the earliest part.
27. **Uncouple:** Let loose to hunt.

HIPPOLYTA.

    I was with Hercules and Cadmus[28] once
    When in a wood of Crete they bayed[29] the bear
    With hounds of Sparta.[30] Never did I hear
120   Such gallant chiding,[31] for, besides the groves,
    The skies, the fountains, every region near
    Seemed all one mutual cry. I never heard
    So musical a discord, such sweet thunder.

THESEUS.

    My hounds are bred out of the Spartan kind,
125   So flewed, so sanded;[32] and their heads are hung
    With ears that sweep away the morning dew,
    Crook-kneed and dewlapped[33] like Thessalian
      bulls;
    Slow in pursuit, but matched in mouth like bells,
130   Each under each.[34] A cry more tuneable[35]
    Was never holloed to, nor cheered with horn,
    In Crete, in Sparta, nor in Thessaly.
    Judge when you hear.—But, soft![36] What nymphs
    are these?

EGEUS.

135   My lord, this is my daughter here asleep,
    And this Lysander; this Demetrius is,
    This Helena, old Nedar's Helena.
    I wonder of their being here together.

THESEUS.

    No doubt they rose up early to observe
140   The rite of May, and hearing our intent,

---

28. Cadmus: In legends, the founder of the city of Thebes.
29. bayed: Brought to bay.
30. hounds of Sparta: Referring to the superior hunting skills of Spartan hounds.
31. chiding: Yelping; barking.
32. So flewed, so sanded: Again, like those of Sparta, with sandy coat and extra, folded flesh around the mouth.
33. dewlapped: Having many folds of skin under the neck.
34. but matched . . . each: With cries arranged like a musical scale, ranging in order from treble to bass notes.
35. cry more tunable: A melodious pack of hounds.
36. soft: Stop.

Came here in grace of our solemnity.[37]
But speak, Egeus. Is not this the day
That Hermia should give answer of her choice?

EGEUS. It is, my lord.

THESEUS.

145   Go, bid the huntsmen wake them with their horns.

A Servant exits.
Shout within. Wind horns. They all start up.

THESEUS.
Good morrow, friends. Saint Valentine[38] is past.
Begin these woodbirds but to couple now?

Demetrius, Helena, Hermia, and Lysander kneel.

LYSANDER.
Pardon, my lord.

THESEUS.   I pray you all, stand up.

They rise.

150   I know you two are rival enemies.
How comes this gentle concord in the world,
That hatred is so far from jealousy[39]
To sleep by hate and fear no enmity?

LYSANDER.
My lord, I shall reply amazèdly,[40]
155   Half sleep, half waking. But as yet, I swear,
I cannot truly say how I came here.
But, as I think— for truly would I speak,
And now I do bethink me, so it is:
I came with Hermia hither. Our intent
160   Was to be gone from Athens, where we might,
Without[41] the peril of the Athenian law—

37. **grace . . . solemnity:** To honor our ritual, our celebration; perhaps of May Day, perhaps of their wedding.
38. **Saint Valentine:** The day when birds were thought to choose their mates.
39. **jealousy:** Suspicion.
40. **amazèdly:** In confusion, as when in a maze.
41. **Without:** Beyond; outside of.

EGEUS.

Enough, enough!—My lord, you have enough.
I beg the law, the law, upon his head.
They would have stol'n away,—They would,
165   Demetrius,
Thereby to have defeated[42] you and me:
You of your wife and me of my consent,
Of my consent that she should be your wife.

DEMETRIUS.

My lord, fair Helen told me of their stealth,
170   Of this their purpose hither[43] to this wood,
And I in fury hither[44] followed them,
Fair Helena in fancy following me.
But, my good lord, I wot not by what power
But by some power it is my love to Hermia,
175   Melted as the snow, seems to me now
As the remembrance of an idle gaud[45]
Which in my childhood I did dote upon,
And all the faith, the virtue[46] of my heart,
The object and the pleasure of mine eye,
180   Is only Helena. To her, my lord,
Was I betrothed ere I saw Hermia.
But, like a sickness,[47] did I loathe this food.
But, as in health, come to my natural taste,
Now I do wish it, love it, long for it,
185   And will forevermore be true to it.

THESEUS.

Fair lovers, you are fortunately met.
Of this discourse we more will hear anon.—
Egeus, I will overbear your will,
For in the temple by and by, with us,
190   These couples shall eternally be knit.—

---

42. defeated: Cheated; defrauded.
43. hither: In the first use, meaning "to come here." In the second use, meaning just "here."
44. in fancy: In love.
45. idle gaud: Worthless trinket.
46. virtue: Power.
47. like a sickness: Like someone who is sick.

And, for[48] the morning now is something[49] worn,
Our purposed hunting shall be set aside.
Away with us to Athens. Three and three,
We'll hold a feast in great solemnity.
195   Come, Hippolyta.

Theseus and his train,
including Hippolyta and Egeus, exit.

DEMETRIUS.
These things seem small and undistinguishable,
Like far-off mountains turnèd into clouds.

HERMIA.
Methinks I see these things with parted eye,[50]
When everything seems double.

200   **HELENA.**   So methinks.
And I have found Demetrius like a jewel,
Mine own and not mine own.[51]

DEMETRIUS.   Are you sure
That we are awake? It seems to me
205   That yet we sleep, we dream. Do not you think
The Duke was here and bid us follow him?

HERMIA.
Yea, and my father.

HELENA.   And Hippolyta.

LYSANDER.
And he did bid us follow to the temple.

DEMETRIUS.
210   Why, then, we are awake. Let's follow him,
And by the way let us recount our dreams.

Lovers exit.

BOTTOM. *(waking up)* When my cue comes, call me, and I
will answer. My next is "Most fair Pyramus." Hey-ho!

48. **for:** Since
49. **something:** A little bit.
50. **parted:** Blurred because divided.
51. **like . . . own:** Helena likens Demetrius to a jewel, found by chance but not
properly owned.

215 Peter Quince! Flute the bellows-mender! Snout the tinker! Starveling! God's my life,[52] Stolen hence, and left me asleep! I have had a most rare vision. I have had a dream, past the wit of man to say what dream it was. Man is but an ass if he go about[53] to expound this dream. Methought I was—there is no man can
220 tell what. Methought I was and methought I had— but man is but a patched[54] fool if he will offer to say what methought I had. The eye of man hath not heard, the ear of man hath not seen, man's hand is not able to taste, his tongue to conceive, nor his
225 heart to report what my dream was.[55] I will get Peter Quince to write a ballad of this dream. It shall be called "Bottom's Dream," because it hath no bottom; and I will sing it in the latter end of a play, before the Duke. Peradventure, to make it the more gracious, I
230 shall sing it at her death.[56]

He exits.

Scene ii. *Enter Quince, Flute, Snout, and Starveling.*

QUINCE. Have you sent to Bottom's house? Is he come home yet?

STARVELING. He cannot be heard of. Out of doubt he is transported.[1]

5 **FLUTE.** If he come not, then the play is marred. It goes not forward, doth it?

QUINCE. It is not possible. You have not a man in all Athens able to discharge[2] Pyramus but he.

---

52. God's my life!: Possibly, God bless or save my life.
53. go about: Attempt; try.
54. patched: Dressed like a jester, in patched clothing.
55. The eye . . . was: Bottom refers to a passage from the Bible's Corinthians 2:9 but recalls it incorrectly.
56. her death: Possibly, the death of Thisbe in the play.
1. transported: Transformed; possibly, carried away by fairies.
2. discharge: Perform; play.

FLUTE. No, he hath simply the best wit of any handi-
10 craftman in Athens.

QUINCE. Yea, and the best person[3] too, and he is a very paramour for a sweet voice.

FLUTE. You must say "paragon." A paramour is God bless us a thing of naught.[4]

Enter Snug the joiner.

15 **SNUG.** Masters, the Duke is coming from the temple, and there is two or three lords and ladies more married. If our sport had gone forward, we had all been made men.[5]

FLUTE. O sweet bully Bottom! Thus hath he lost six
20 pence a day during his life. He could not have scaped six pence a day. An the Duke had not given him six pence a day[6] for playing Pyramus, I'll be hanged. He would have deserved it. Six pence a day in Pyramus, or nothing!

Enter Bottom.

25 **BOTTOM.** Where are these lads? Where are these hearts?[7]

QUINCE. Bottom! O most courageous day! O most happy hour!

BOTTOM. Masters, I am to discourse wonders But ask
30 me not what; for, if I tell you, I am not true Athenian. I will tell you everything right as it fell out.

QUINCE. Let us hear, sweet Bottom.

BOTTOM. Not a word of me.[8] All that I will tell you is that the Duke hath dined. Get your apparel to-
35 gether, good strings to your beards,[9] new ribbons

---

3. **best person:** Best presentation or appearance.
4. **a thing of naught:** A shameful or wicked thing.
5. **we . . . men:** We would be men whose fortunes were made.
6. **six pence a day:** As a pension would give.
7. **hearts:** Fellows of good heart.
8. **of me:** From me.
9. **strings to your beards:** Ties to hold on their false beards.

to your pumps.[10] Meet presently[11] at the palace. Every man look o'er his part. For the short and the long is, our play is preferred.[12] In any case, let Thisbe have clean linen, and let not him that plays the lion pare his nails, for they shall hang out for the lion's claws. And, most dear actors, eat no onions nor garlic, for we are to utter sweet breath, and I do not doubt but to hear them say it is a sweet comedy. No more words. Away! Go, away!

They exit.

10. pumps: Dress-up shoes.
11. presently: Now; right away.
12. preferred: Selected; recommended.

Act V

Scene i. *Enter Theseus, Hippolyta, and Philostrate, Lords, and Attendants*

HIPPOLYTA.

'Tis strange, my Theseus, that[1] these lovers speak of.

THESEUS.

More strange than true. I never may[2] believe
These antique fables,[3] nor these fairy toys.[4]
5   Lovers and madmen have such seething brains,
Such shaping fantasies, that apprehend[5]
More than cool reason ever comprehends.
The lunatic, the lover, and the poet
Are of imagination all compact.[6]
10   One sees more devils than vast hell can hold:
That is the madman. The lover, all as frantic,
Sees Helen's beauty in a brow of Egypt.[7]
The poet's eye, in a fine frenzy rolling,
Doth glance from heaven to earth, from earth to
15   heaven,
And as imagination bodies forth
The forms of things unknown, the poet's pen
Turns them to shapes, and gives to airy nothing
A local habitation and a name.
20   Such tricks hath strong imagination
That, if it would but apprehend some joy,

---

1. that: What.
2. may: Can.
3. antique fables: Old and possibly "antic," or strange.
4. fairy toys: Silly tales about fairies.
5. shaping . . . apprehend: Creative imaginations that conceive.
6. of imagination all compact: Created entirely by fantasy.
7. Helen's beauty . . . Egypt: This means a lover sees beauty such as that of supremely beautiful Helen of Troy even in a dark Gypsy's face (thought to be unattractive in Shakespeare's time).

It comprehends[8] some bringer[9] of that joy.
Or in the night, imagining some fear,[10]
How easy is a bush supposed a bear!

HIPPOLYTA.

25   But all the story of the night told over,
And all their minds transfigured so together,
More witnesseth than fancy's images[11]
And grows to something of great constancy,[12]
But, howsoever,[13] strange and admirable.[14]

*Enter Lovers: Lysander, Demetrius,
Hermia, and Helena.*

THESEUS.

30   Here come the lovers full of joy and mirth.—
Joy, gentle friends! Joy and fresh days of love
Accompany your hearts!

LYSANDER.   More than to us
Wait in your royal walks, your board, your bed!

THESEUS.

35   Come now; what masques,[15] what dances shall we
have
To wear away this long age of three hours
Between our after-supper[16] and bedtime?
Where is our usual manager of mirth?

40   What revels are in hand? Is there no play
To ease the anguish of a torturing hour?
Call Philostrate.

PHILOSTRATE. *(coming forward)*
Here, mighty Theseus.

---

8. comprehends: Includes.
9. bringer: The source of.
10. fear: Object of fear.
11. More . . . images: Confirms something beyond fantasy.
12. constancy: Reliability; consistency.
13. howsoever: In any case.
14. admirable: Worth admiring.
15. masques: Masked entertainment for the court, similar to the **revels** mentioned in line 39.
16. after-supper: Snack served after an early evening meal.

THESEUS.

    Say what abridgment[17] have you for this evening,
45   What masque, what music? How shall we beguile
    The lazy time if not with some delight?

PHILOSTRATE. *(giving Theseus a paper)*
    There is a brief how many sports are ripe.[18]
    Make choice of which your Highness will see first.

THESEUS.

    "The battle with the Centaurs,[19] to be sung
50   By an Athenian eunuch to the harp."
    We'll none of that. That have I told my love
    In glory of my kinsman[20] Hercules.
    "The riot of the tipsy Bacchanals,
    Tearing the Thracian singer in their rage."[21]
55   That is an old device,[22] and it was played
    When I from Thebes came last a conqueror.
    "The thrice-three muses mourning for the death
    Of learning, late deceased in beggary."[23]
    That is some satire, keen and critical,
60   Not sorting with[24] a nuptial ceremony.
    "A tedious brief scene of young Pyramus
    And his love Thisbe, very tragical mirth."
    "Merry" and tragical? "Tedious" and "brief"?
    That is hot ice and wondrous strange snow!
65   How shall we find the concord of this discord?

PHILOSTRATE.

    A play there is, my lord, some ten words long,
    Which is as brief as I have known a play,

17. abridgment: Device, such as a game or entertainment, to shorten, or abridge, the evening's time.
18. brief . . . ripe: A summary of the entertainments available.
19. battle . . . Centaurs: Refers to an incident in Hercules' life.
20. my kinsman: In Plutarch's "Life of Theseus," Hercules and Theseus are cousins.
21. The riot . . . rage: This refers to the the death of Orpheus, the Thracian singer, as told in *Metamorphoses 9.*
22. device: Play; entertainment.
23. The thrice . . . beggary: Refers to satirical plays criticizing the neglect for culture and scholarship; specifically the **thrice-three,** or nine, **Muses** watched over such learning and creativity.
24. sorting with: Appropriate for.

But by ten words, my lord, it is too long,
Which makes it tedious; for in all the play,
70 There is not one word apt, one player fitted.
And tragical, my noble lord, it is.
For Pyramus therein doth kill himself,
Which, when I saw rehearsed, I must confess,
Made mine eyes water; but more merry tears
75 The passion[25] of loud laughter never shed.

THESEUS.
What are they that do play it?

PHILOSTRATE.
Hard-handed men that work in here,
Which never labored in their minds till now;
And now have toiled[26] their unbreathed[27] memories
80 With this same play, against[28] your nuptial.

THESEUS.
And we will hear it.

PHILOSTRATE.   No, my noble lord,
It is not for you. I have heard it over,
And it is nothing, nothing in the world,
85 Unless you can find sport in their intents,
Extremely stretched and conned[29] with cruel pain
To do you service.

THESEUS.   I will hear that play,
For never anything can be amiss
90 When simpleness[30] and duty tender it.
Go, bring them in—and take your places, ladies.

Philostrate exits.

HIPPOLYTA. I love not to see wretchedness o'er charged,[31]
And duty in his[32] service perishing.

25. **passion:** Intense.
26. **toiled:** Exhausted.
27. **unbreathed:** Unexercised.
28. **against:** In preparation for.
29. **conned:** Learned by heart; memorized.
30. **simpleness:** Simplicity; unsophistication.
31. **wretchedness o'ercharged:** Overburdened wretches, or people of low social status.
32. **his:** Its.

THESEUS.
Why, gentle sweet, you shall see no such thing.

HIPPOLYTA.
95   He says they can do nothing in this kind.

THESEUS.
    The kinder we, to give them thanks for nothing.
    Our sport shall be to take what they mistake;
    And what poor duty cannot do, noble respect
    Takes it in might, not merit.[33]
100   Where I have come, great clerks[34] have purposèd
    To greet me with premeditated welcomes,
    Where I have seen them shiver and look pale,
    Make periods in the midst of sentences,
    Throttle their practiced accent[35] in their fears,
105   And in conclusion dumbly have broke off,
    Not paying me a welcome. Trust me, sweet,
    Out of this silence yet I picked a welcome,
    And in the modesty of fearful duty,
    I read as much as from the rattling tongue
110   Of saucy and audacious eloquence.
    Love, therefore, and tongue-tied simplicity
    In least speak most, to my capacity.[36]

Enter Philostrate.

PHILOSTRATE.
So please your Grace, the Prologue is addressed.[37]

THESEUS. Let him approach.

Enter the Prologue.

PROLOGUE.
115   If we offend, it is with our goodwill.
      That you should think we come not to offend,
    But with goodwill. To show our simple skill,

---

33. Takes . . . merit: Considers the effort, not just the result.
34. clerks: Scholars.
35. their practiced accent: The way they had practiced speaking or, possibly, the way they usually spoke.
36. to my capacity: As I see it; in my view.
37. addressed: Ready.

That is the true beginning of our end.[38]
Consider then, we come but in despite.
120   We do not come, as minding[39] to content you,
Our true intent is. All for your delight
We are not here. That you should here repent
    you,
The actors are at hand, and, by their show,
125   You shall know all that you are like to know,

Prologue exits.

THESEUS. This fellow doth not stand upon points.[40]

LYSANDER. He hath rid his prologue like a rough colt; he
knows not the stop.[41] A good moral, my lord: it is
not enough to speak, but to speak true.

130   **HIPPOLYTA.** Indeed he hath played on this prologue like
a child on a recorder[42]—a sound, but not in government.[43]

THESEUS. His speech was like a tangled chain—nothing[44] impaired, but all disordered. Who is next?

*Enter Pyramus (Bottom), and Thisbe (Flute), and Wall
(Snout), and Moonshine (Starveling), and Lion (Snug),
and Prologue (Quince).*

QUINCE. *(as Prologue)*
135   Gentles, perchance you wonder at this show.
    But wonder on, till truth make all things plain.
This man is Pyramus, if you would know.
    This beauteous lady Thisbe is certain.
This man with lime and roughcast, doth present
140   "Wall", that vile wall which did these lovers sun-
    der;

38. end: Goal; aim.
39. minding: Intending.
40. stand upon points: A figure of speech meaning both "is unconcerned
about detail"; and "doesn't care about punctuation (as in points or periods)."
41. rid . . . the stop: He has dashed through his prologue like the rider of an
unbroken colt who cannot be stopped. *Stop* also refers to the punctuation of a
period, which stops the sentence and speaker.
42. recorder: A small wind instrument.
43. government: Control.
44. nothing: Not at all.

And through Walls chink, poor souls, they are content
  To whisper, at the which let no man wonder.
145 This man, with lantern, dog, and bush of thorn,
  Presenteth "Moonshine"; for, if you will know,
By moonshine did these lovers think no scorn
  To meet at Ninus' tomb, there, there to woo.
This grisly beast which "Lion" hight[45] by name
150 The trusty Thisbe coming first by night
Did scare away, or rather did affright;
  And, as she fled, her mantle she did fall[46]
Which Lion vile with bloody mouth did stain.
Anon comes Pyramus, sweet youth and tall,[47]
155 And finds his trusty Thisbe's mantle slain.
Whereat, with blade, with bloody blameful blade,
  He bravely broached[48] his boiling bloody breast.
And Thisbe, tarrying in mulberry shade,
  His dagger drew, and died. For all the rest,
160 Let Lion, Moonshine, Wall, and lovers twain,
At large[49] discourse, while here they do remain.

THESEUS. I wonder if the lion be to speak.

DEMETRIUS. No wonder, my lord: One lion may when many asses do.

    Lion, Thisbe, Moonshine, and Prologue exit.

SNOUT. *(as Wall)*
165 In this same interlude it doth befall
That I, one Snout by name, present a wall;
And such a wall as I would have you think
That had in it a crannied hole or chink,
Through which the lovers, Pyramus and Thisbe,
170 Did whisper often, very secretly.
This loam, this roughcast, and this stone doth show
That I am that same wall. The truth is so.

---

45. hight: Is called.
46. fall: Let fall; drop.
47. tall: Courageous; brave.
48. broached: Stabbed.
49. At large: At length.

And this the cranny is, right and sinister,[50]
175   Through which the fearful lovers are to whisper.

THESEUS. Would you desire lime and hair to speak
better?

DEMETRIUS. It is the wittiest partition[51] that ever I heard
discourse, my lord.

180 **THESEUS.** Pyramus draws near the wall. Silence.

BOTTOM. *(as Pyramus)*
O grim-looked night! O night with hue so black!
O night, which ever art when day is not!
O night! O night! Alack, alack, alack!
I fear my Thisbe's promise is forgot.
185   And thou, O wall, O sweet, O lovely wall,
That stand'st between her father's ground and
mine;
Thou wall, O wall, O sweet and lovely wall,
Show me thy chink, to blink through with mine
190   eyne.
Thanks, courteous wall. Jove shield thee well for
this!
But what see I? No Thisbe do I see.
O wicked wall, through whom I see no bliss,
195   Cursed be thy stones for thus deceiving me!

THESEUS. The wall, methinks, being sensible,[52] should
curse again.[53]

PYRAMUS. No, in truth, sir, he should not. "Deceiving
me" is Thisbe's cue. She is to enter now, and I am
200   to spy her through the wall. You shall see it will fall
pat[54] as I told you. Yonder she comes.

Enter Thisbe (Flute).

---

50. right and sinister: Literally, running right and left. *Left* is **sinister** because
on Judgment Day, those sent to Hell are directed to the left at the Gates of
Heaven.
51. wittiest partition: Most intelligent wall; also section of a speech.
52. sensible: Conscious; aware.
53. curse again: Curse in return.
54. fall pat: Occur exactly.

FLUTE. *(as Thisbe)*
> O wall, full often hast thou heard my moans
> For parting my fair Pyramus and me.
> My cherry lips have often kissed thy stones,
205   Thy stones with lime and hair knit up in thee.

BOTTOM. *(as Pyramus)*
> I see a voice! Now will I to the chink
> To spy[55] an I can hear my Thisbe's face.
> Thisbe?

FLUTE. *(as Thisbe)*
> My love! Thou art my love, I think.

BOTTOM. *(as Pyramus)*
210   Think what thou wilt, I am thy lover's grace,[56]
> And, like Limander,[57] am I trusty still.

FLUTE. *(as Thisbe)*
> And I like Helen,[58] till the Fates me kill.

BOTTOM. *(as Pyramus)*
> Not Shafalus to Procrus[59] was so true.

FLUTE. *(as Thisbe)*
> As Shafalus to Procrus, I to you.

BOTTOM. *(as Pyramus)*
215   O kiss me through the hole of this vile wall.

FLUTE. *(as Thisbe)*
> I kiss the wall's hole, not your lips at all.

BOTTOM. *(as Pyramus)*
> Wilt thou at Ninny's tomb meet me straightway?

FLUTE. *(as Thisbe)*
> 'Tide[60] life, 'tide death, I come without delay.

Bottom and Flute exit.

55. an: If.
56. thy lover's grace: Your gracious lover.
57. Limander: Bottom means the famous lover Leander, but he has confused the name.
58. Helen: Again, Bottom probably means Hero, Leander's lover.
59. Shafalus to Procrus: Again, Bottom probably means the famous lovers Cephalus and Procris.
60. 'Tide: Contraction for *Betide,* meaning "come."

SNOUT. *(as Wall)*
Thus have I, Wall, my part dischargèd so,
220   And, being done, thus Wall away doth go. *(He exits.)*

THESEUS. Now is the wall down between the two neighbors.

DEMETRIUS. No remedy, my lord, when walls are so wilful to hear without warning.

225 **HIPPOLYTA.** This is the silliest stuff that ever I heard.

THESEUS. The best in this kind[61] are but shadows,[62] and the worst are no worse, if imagination amend them.

HIPPOLYTA. It must be your imagination then, and not
230   theirs.

THESEUS. If we imagine no worse of them than they of themselves, they may pass for excellent men. Here come two noble beasts in, a man and a lion.

Enter Lion (Snug) and Moonshine (Starveling).

SNUG. *(as Lion)*
You, ladies, you whose gentle hearts do fear
235   The smallest monstrous mouse that creeps on
      floor,
May now perchance both quake and tremble here,
When lion rough in wildest rage doth roar.
Then know that I, as Snug the joiner, am
240   A lion fell,[63] nor else no lion's dam;
For if I should as lion come in strife
Into this place, 'twere pity on my life.

THESEUS. A very gentle beast, and of a good conscience.

DEMETRIUS. The very best at a beast, my lord, that e'er I
245   saw.

LYSANDER. This lion is a very fox for his valor.

THESEUS. True, and a goose for his discretion.

61. **in this kind:** In plays of this type; with players of this sort.
62. **shadows:** Illusions; representations.
63. **lion fell:** Fierce lion, possibly with second meaning of "skin" for **fell**.

DEMETRIUS. Not so, my lord, for his valor cannot carry his discretion, and the fox carries the goose.

250 **THESEUS.** His discretion, I am sure, cannot carry his valor; for the goose carries not the fox. It is well. Leave it to his discretion, and let us listen to the Moon.

STARVELING. *(as Moonshine)*
This lanthorn doth the hornèd moon present.

255 **DEMETRIUS.** He should have worn the horns on his head.

THESEUS. He is no crescent, and his horns are invisible within the circumference.

STARVELING. *(as Moonshine)*
This lanthorn[64] doth the hornèd moon present.
260 Myself the Man i' th' Moon do seem to be.

THESEUS. This is the greatest error of all the rest; the man should be put into the lanthorn. How is it else "the man i' th' moon"?

DEMETRIUS. He dares not come there for[65] the candle,
265 for you see, it is already in snuff.[66]

HIPPOLYTA. I am aweary of this moon. Would he would change.

THESEUS. It appears by his small light of discretion that he is in the wane; but yet, in courtesy, in all rea-
270 son, we must stay the time.

LYSANDER. Proceed, Moon.

STARVELING. *(as Moonshine)* All that I have to say is to tell you that the lanthorn is the moon; I the man i' th' Moon this thornbush my thornbush, and this
275 dog my dog.

---

64. lanthorn: Literally, *lantern* but possibly a play on the horns a cuckold wears (referred to further in lines 254–255) and the horns of which lanterns were then commonly made.
65. for: Because he fears.
66. in snuff: Upset; angry or needing to be snuffed; i.e., needing its wick trimmed.

DEMETRIUS. Why, all these should be in the lanthorn for all these are in the moon. But silence. Here comes Thisbe.

Enter Thisbe (Flute)

FLUTE. *(as Thisbe)*
This is old Ninny's tomb. Where is my love?

280 **SNUG.** *(as Lion) O!*

*The Lion roars. Thisbe runs off,
dropping her mantle.*

DEMETRIUS. Well roared, Lion.

THESEUS. Well run, Thisbe.

HIPPOLYTA. Well shone, Moon. Truly, the Moon shines with a good grace.

Lion worries the mantle.

285 **THESEUS.** Well moused,[67] Lion.

Enter Pyramus (Bottom)

DEMETRIUS. And then came Pyramus.

Lion exits.

LYSANDER. And so the lion vanished.

BOTTOM. *(as Pyramus)*
Sweet Moon, I thank thee for thy sunny beams.
I thank thee, Moon, for shining now so bright,
290 For by thy gracious, golden, glittering gleams,
I trust to take of truest Thisbe sight.—
But stay! O spite!
But mark, poor knight,
What dreadful dole[68] is here!
295 Eyes, do you see!
How can it be!
O dainty duck! O dear!
Thy mantle good—
What, stained with blood?

---

67. **moused:** Torn and shaken as a cat would a mouse.
68. **dole:** Sad or upsetting event or thing.

300   Approach, ye Furies[69] fell![70]
O Fates,[71] come, come,
Cut thread and thrum,[72]
Quail,[73] crush, conclude, and quell![74]

THESEUS. This passion, and the death of a dear friend,
305   would go near to make a man look sad.

HIPPOLYTA. Beshrew[75] my heart but I pity the man.

BOTTOM. *(as Pyramus)*
O wherefore, Nature, didst thou lions frame,
Since lion vile hath here deflowered my dear,
Which is—no, no—which was the fairest dame
310   That lived, that loved, that liked, that looked with cheer?[76]
Come, tears, confound!
Out, sword, and wound
The pap of Pyramus;
315   Ay, that left pap,[77]
Where heart doth hop.   *(Pyramus stabs himself)*
Thus die I, thus, thus, thus.
Now am I dead;
Now am I fled;
320   My soul is in the sky.
Tongue, lose thy light!
Moon, take thy flight!   *(Moonshine exits.)*
Now die, die, die, die, die.   *(Pyramus falls.)*

69. Furies: In Greek mythology, those who broke natural or moral laws were avenged by the Furies.
70. fell: Fierce.
71. Fates: Three mythological Greek goddesses who controlled human life and death by weaving and cutting its threads.
72. thread and thrum: Thread refers to Pyramus' whole life, while the thrum refers to the loose end of the warp thread (one of the threads in weaving).
73. Quail: Overwhelm; destroy.
74. quell: Kill.
75. Beshrew: Curse.
76. cheer: Face; countenance.
77. pap: Breast.

DEMETRIUS. No die,[78] but an ace,[79] for him, for he is but
325   one.

LYSANDER. Less than an ace, man, for he is dead, he is
    nothing.

THESEUS. With the help of a surgeon he might yet re-
    cover and yet prove an ass.[80]

330 **HIPPOLYTA.** How chance[81] Moonshine is gone before
    Thisbe comes back and finds her lover?

THESEUS. She will find him by starlight.

Enter Thisbe (Flute).

Here she comes, and her passion ends the play.

HIPPOLYTA. Methinks she should not use a long one for
335   such a Pyramus. I hope she will be brief.

DEMETRIUS. A mote will turn the balance, which Pyra-
    mus, which Thisbe, is the better; he for a man, God
    warrant us; she for a woman, God bless us.

LYSANDER. She hath spied him already with those sweet
340   eyes.

DEMETRIUS. And thus she means,[82] *videlicet*[83]—

FLUTE. *(as Thisbe)*
        Asleep, my love?
        What, dead, my dove?
        O Pyramus, arise!
345   Speak, speak. Quite dumb?
        Dead? dead? A tomb
    Must cover thy sweet eyes.
        These lily lips,
        This cherry nose,

---

78. die: Singular of dice, but also a pun on Pyramus' on-stage death.
79. ace: A one-spot side on a die. Here, Demetrius is saying Bottom's perfor-
mance is worth only one side of a die, not even the whole die.
80. ass: A pun on *ace*.
81. How chance: How did it happen that.
82. means: Moans.
83. *videlicet*: Therefore; thus follows; to wit.

350   These yellow cowslip cheeks
             Are gone, are gone!
             Lovers, make moan;
         His eyes were green as leeks.
             O Sisters Three,[84]
355   Come, come to me
         With hands as pale as milk.
             Lay them in gore,
             Since you have shore[85]
         With shears his thread of silk.
360   Tongue, not a word!
             Come, trusty sword,
         Come, blade, my breast imbrue.[86]

                                Thisbe stabs herself.

         And farewell, friends.
         Thus Thisbe ends.
365   Adieu, adieu, adieu.   *(Thisbe falls.)*

THESEUS. Moonshine and Lion are left to bury the dead.

DEMETRIUS. Ay, and Wall too.

                                Bottom and Flute arise.

BOTTOM. No, I assure you, the wall is down that parted
their fathers. Will it please you to see the Epilogue
370 or to hear a Bergomask dance[87] between two of our
company?

THESEUS. No epilogue, I pray you; for your play needs
no excuse. Never excuse. For when the players are
all dead, there need none to be blamed. Marry, if
375 he that writ it had played Pyramus and hanged
himself in Thisbe's garter, it would have been a fine
tragedy; and so it is, truly, and very notably dis-
charged. But come, your Bergomask. Let your epilogue alone.

84. Sisters Three: A reference back to the Fates from line 300.
85. shore: A spelling variation for *shorn*, meaning "cut," used to rhyme with *gore*.
86. imbrue: Wet with blood.
87. Bergomask dance: A country dance originating in Venice, Italy.

Dance, and the players exit.

380   The iron tongue of midnight[88] hath told[89] twelve.
Lovers, to bed! 'Tis almost fairy time.
I fear we shall outsleep the coming morn
As much as we this night have overwatched.[90]
This palpable-gross[91] play hath well beguiled
385   The heavy[92] gait of night. Sweet friends, to bed.
A fortnight hold we this solemnity
In nightly revels and new jollity.   *(They exit.)*

Enter Robin Goodfellow.

ROBIN.

     Now the hungry lion roars,
       And the wolf behowls the moon,
390   Whilst the heavy[93] plowman snores,
       All with weary task fordone.[94]
     Now the wasted brands[95] do glow,
       Whilst the screech-owl, screeching loud,
     Puts the wretch that lies in woe
395   In remembrance of a shroud.
     Now it is the time of night
       That the graves, all gaping wide,
     Every one lets forth his sprite
       In the church-way paths to glide.
400   And we fairies, that do run
       By the triple Hecate's[96] team
     From the presence of the sun,
       Following darkness like a dream,
     Now are frolic.[97] Not a mouse
405   Shall disturb this hallowed house.

---

88. iron tongue of midnight: The bell rung at midnight.
89. told: Has tolled or rung.
90. overwatched: Stayed up so late.
91. palpable-gross: Clearly gross and crude.
92. heavy: Slow.
93. heavy: Weary.
94. foredone: Tired; worn out.
95. wasted brands: Burned-up firewood.
96. triple Hecate: The mythological goddess Hecate had three forms, with a name for each: in the sky she was Luna, the moon; on earth, she was Diana; in the underworld, she was Proserpina.
97. frolic: Playful; happy.

I am sent with broom before,
To sweep the dust behind[98] the door.

Enter Oberon and Titania, King and Queen of Fairies,
with all their train.

OBERON.
Through the house give glimmering light,
By the dead and drowsy fire.
410   Every elf and fairy sprite,
Hop as light as bird from brier,
And this ditty after me,
Sing and dance it trippingly.

TITANIA.
First rehearse your song by rote,
415   To each word a warbling note.
Hand in hand, with fairy grace,
Will we sing and bless this place.

Oberon leads the Fairies in song and dance.

OBERON.
Now, until the break of day,
Through this house each fairy stray.
420   To the best bride-bed will we,
Which by us shall blessèd be,
And the issue there create[99]
Ever shall be fortunate.
So shall all the couples three
425   Ever true in loving be,
And the blots of Nature's hand
Shall not in their issue stand.
Never mole, harelip, nor scar,
Nor mark prodigious,[100] such as are
430   Despisèd in nativity,
Shall upon their children be.
With this field-dew consecrate[101]

---

98. behind: Collected behind the door. This was a task Puck/Robin Goodfellow might influence as a household sprite.
99. there create: Created there.
100. prodigious: Abnormal; ominous.
101. consecrate: Blessed; sacred.

Every fairy take his gait,[102]
And each several[103] chamber bless,
335 Through this palace, with sweet peace.
And the owner of it blest,
Ever shall in safety rest.
Trip away. Make no stay.
Meet me all by break of day.

All but Robin exit.

ROBIN.
440 If we shadows have offended,
Think but this and all is mended:
That you have but slumbered here
While these visions did appear.
And this weak and idle[104] theme,
445 No more yielding[105] but a dream,
Gentles, do not reprehend.
If you pardon, we will mend.[106]
And, as I am an honest Puck,
If we have unearnèd luck
450 Now to 'scape the serpent's tongue,[107]
We will make amends ere long.
Else the Puck a liar call.
So good night unto you all.
Give me your hands,[108] if we be friends,
455 And Robin shall restore amends.[109]

He exits

102. **take his gait:** Carry on; proceed.
103. **several:** Separate.
104. **idle:** Silly; trivial.
105. **no more yielding:** Yielding, or producing, no more than.
106. **mend:** Make better; improve.
107. **'scape the serpent's tongue:** Escape, or not receive, any hissing from the audience.
108. **Give me your hands:** Clap for us; applaud.
109. **restore amends:** Pay back your applause with satisfaction.